CHRISTINA ROSSETTI: POEMS

Christina Rossetti

AUTHORED by Erika Andersen
UPDATED AND REVISED by A. Boghani

COVER DESIGN by Table XI Partners LLC
COVER PHOTO by Olivia Verma and © 2005 GradeSaver, LLC

BOOK DESIGN by Table XI Partners LLC

Published by GradeSaver LLC, www.gradesaver.com

First published in the United States of America by GradeSaver LLC. 2013

ISBN 978-1-60259-392-3

Printed in the United States of America

For other products and additional information please visit
http://www.gradesaver.com

Table of Contents

Table of Contents

Table of Contents

Biography of Rossetti, Christina (1830-1894)

Christina Georgina Rossetti was born in London on December 5th 1830. She was the fourth child of Gabriele and Frances Rossetti, who already had two sons and a daughter. Gabriele Rossetti had been exiled from Italy for his support of revolutionary nationalism and was now a professor of Italian and a Dante Scholar at King's College in London. His wife, born Frances Polidori, was the English-Italian daughter of John William Polidori, an author and Lord Byron's physician. Although Gabriele was a Roman Catholic, he allowed his wife to raise their children in the Anglican church.

All four Rossetti children developed artistic and literary inclinations; Maria Francesca wrote about Dante Alighieri before becoming an Anglican nun, Dante Gabriel was a poet and painter, and William Michael was a writer and critic as well as a co-founder of the Pre-Raphaelite Brotherhood with Dante Gabriel. Young Christina was not intimidated by her older siblings' success. In fact, she thrived during her childhood in London, where she was always surrounded by visiting scholars, artists, authors, and political firebrands.

At the age of 6, Rossetti started to demonstrate the depth of her own literary talent when she recited an original poem about a young girl named Cecelia and the gladiator who protected her. Frances home-schooled her lively youngest daughter, teaching her about classical and religious literature, fairy tales, novels, and the work of visionaries like Alighieri, Petrarch and Keats. Christina Rossetti had an extremely close relationship with her mother, and inherited Frances's intense religious devotion, which would later permeate her written work. In fact, Rossetti's first published poem was called "To My Mother."

Rossetti wrote "To My Mother" when she was eleven years old, even though it was not until 1847 that her grandfather decided to publish it privately. The years in between proved to be very difficult for the Rossetti family. In 1843, Gabriele began to lose his eyesight and was diagnosed with tuberculosis. He retired from King's College, leaving a financial vacuum that Frances attempted to fill by teaching while Maria worked as a governess. Gabriele Rossetti, meanwhile, suffered from depression until his death in 1854. Because her mother and siblings were working, Christina's life became increasingly isolated and she, too, experienced long bouts of melancholy. In addition to her troubled mind, she also suffered from ill health, further compounded by her hypochondria. Poetry became an outlet for Rossetti to navigate these difficult circumstances. She expressed her morbid thoughts and religious zeal through her writing.

Rossetti was quiet and reserved throughout her adolescence, but she still had a large circle of friends, including three serious suitors. When she was seventeen years old, a man named James Collinson proposed to her. He was a shy, young painter involved in the Pre-Raphaelite Brotherhood. Rossetti accepted, but in 1850, she broke off the engagement because Collinson reverted to Catholicism. Rossetti was a devout follower of Tractarianism, an Anglo-Catholic branch of Christianity. Later, she refused a second marriage proposal from linguist Charles Bagot Cayley, also because of his religious beliefs. Rossetti then refused a third offer of marriage, for unknown reasons, from the painter John Brett.

In 1848, Christina Rossetti made her public debut when two of her poems, "Death's Chill Between" and "Heart's Chill Between," appeared in a magazine called *The Athenaeum*. Later that year, Rossetti began submitting her work for publication in *The Germ*, a journal that her brothers founded during the emergence of the Pre-Raphaelite Brotherhood. She published seven poems under the pseudonym Ellen Alleyne. As a woman, she could not attend Brotherhood meetings, but Christina Rossetti still participated actively in the movement. She was the model for several of her brother Dante's paintings, including *The Girlhood of Mary Virgin* (1849) and *Ecce Ancilla Domini (The Annunciation)* (1850). Christina also tried her hand at painting, but her poetry remains her most significant contribution to the Pre-Raphaelite movement.

Christina Rossetti's innovative use of gothic themes, medievalism, chimerical settings, and Christian symbolism established her as an influential luminary in the Pre-Raphaelite aesthetic. By writing poetry that demanded meticulous reading and interpretation, Rossetti developed a literary counterpart to the Pre-Raphaelite painting method known as "close-looking." In 1862, Rossetti published *Goblin Market and Other Poems*, which critics hailed as the first literary success of the movement. Scholars believe that Rossetti was inspired to choose this title by her involvement with St. Mary Magdalene Home for Fallen Women at Highgate Hill. To this day, though, scholars are still locked in heated debates about the interpretation of the titular poem.

The success of *Goblin Market* led to Rossetti's second collection, *The Prince's Progress and Other Poems* in 1866 followed by *Commonplace and Other Stories*, a set of fairy tales that was published in 1870. However, critics were not quite as impressed by Rossetti's narrative work and encouraged her to return to poetry. She continued to write both poems and fairy tales, and in 1872, she published a didactic nursery rhyme anthology called *Sing-Song*. Lewis Carroll, a friend of the Rossetti family, lauded the poems and the accompanying illustrations. As a way of showing her mutual admiration, Christina Rossetti wrote a second children's book, *Speaking Likenesses*, which resembles of Carroll's nonsense poetry. The three fairytales in *Speaking Likenesses* are quite dark and intended to intimidate young readers. Rossetti often wrote *at* children and not *for* them in order to preach the moral lessons that pervaded Victorian methods of child-rearing. As a result, scholars consider Rossetti's children's stories to be among literature's most terrifying, rivaling the work of the Brothers Grimm. During her time, though, Victorian parents embraced Rossetti's tales because they approved of didactic reading material for their children, even if the children did not like it.

In 1850, Rossetti wrote *Maude: Prose and Verse*, an autobiographical novel about her challenging teenage years. However, her brother William dismissed it as a frivolous tale for young girls, and the novel was not published until three years after Christina Rossetti's death. *Maude* offers fascinating insight into the mind of the young Rossetti, who was zealous in her spiritual devotion and morosely obsessed with the reflection of her sins. Rossetti had suffered from ill health all of her life, both physical and mental. In 1871, she was diagnosed with Grave's Disease, and her symptoms included protruding eyes and the discoloration of her skin. In 1893, she developed breast cancer and died a year later, on December 29th 1894. She is buried in the Highgate Cemetery.

Although her older brother William described Christina as the least bookish member of their literary family, scholars consider Christina Rossetti to be one of the finest poets of the Victorian era. She helped to define the Pre-Raphaelite movement. Like Elizabeth Barrett Browning before her, Rossetti made an impression on a literary world saturated with male voices with her thought-provoking symbolism and deep questioning of human mortality. Today, her work is studied and celebrated by a wide audience, often through her original lyrics for well-known Christmas carols. Although she was appreciated during her lifetime, Christina Rossetti's enduring legacy has had a major impact on twentieth-century feminist critique.

About Christina Rossetti: Poems

Scholars widely acknowledge Christina Rossetti as one of the greatest Victorian poets and the foremost poet of the Pre-Raphaelite Brotherhood. She excelled in using words to invoke the particular aesthetic of the movement. She based some of her work on her own life experiences and observations of nature, but more commonly, Rossetti wrote about about her thoughts on mortality and spiritual existence.

In 1848, *The Athenaeum*, the leading weekly literary journal of that time, published two of Rossetti's poems. Her elder brother, Dante Gabriele, suggested the titles: "Death's Chill Between" and "Heart's Chill Between." These poems focus on the theme of unrequited love, which is common in Pre-Raphaelite art and in Rossetti's body of work. However, young Rossetti had very little experience in love, and almost certainly drew inspiration from literature and her own lively imagination. Later in her career, Rossetti's devotional poems became more autobiographical, but in this instance, she expresses fictional emotions. In her early work, though, Rossetti is able to invoke her young female protagonist's pain in a deep, visceral way. Rossetti also contributed seven poems to *The Germ*, the official journal of the Pre-Raphaelite Brotherhood. Unfortunately, the periodical folded after publishing only 4 issues.

Meanwhile, Rossetti's singular talent caught the attention of other publications. In 1859, *Once a Week* Magazine published "Maude Clare," another tale of thwarted love. Rossetti had composed "Maude Clare," which was originally forty-one stanzas long, between 1857 and 1858. However, *Once a Week* only printed fifteen stanzas and when the poem was published as part of *Goblin Market and Other Poems*, the publishers cut out three additional stanzas. In Rossetti's original manuscript, Maude Clare is a much more sympathetic character than in the published versions. This is because the extra stanzas explain her behavior in church and reveal a softer side to Maude's femme fatale persona.

In 1861, the literary periodical *MacMillan's Magazine* published "Up-Hill," which Rossetti had penned in 1858. The poem became extremely popular among readers, leading the magazine to publish several more. Later that year, MacMillan's published "A Birthday" (1857). Although MacMillan's was founded in 1859, Rossetti's work helped to propel its readership, making it into a leading intellectual journal. Concurrently, Rossetti's readership expanded significantly as a result of her relationship with the magazine.

In 1862, Rossetti's collection *Goblin Men and Other Poems* was published. Rossetti wrote the titular poem, originally titled "A Peep at Goblin Men" in 1859. "Goblin Market" turned out to be her most celebrated poem (as well as her longest). Rossetti dedicated the poem to her sister Maria as a way of paying tribute to their bond. The content was likely inspired by Rossetti's work at the St. Mary Magdalene Highgate Home for Fallen Women, where she ministered to reformed prostitutes. While

Rossetti claimed that she never meant for "Goblin Market" to have any underlying moral messages, scholars argue that the piece holds both Christian and feminist implications. Out of Rossetti's entire body of work, "Goblin Market" remains her most widely studied poem. It launched her literary career, and in turn, inspired Lewis Carroll to write *Alice's Adventures in Wonderland.*

Among the non-devotional pieces in *Goblin Market and Other Poems* is "Remember," a poem that Rossetti penned in 1849. This sonnet also regularly appears in school curricula because of its elegiac nature and Rossetti's deep exploration of human existence and mortality. Rossetti had always been deeply religious, but in 1845, the Park Village Sisterhood, the First Anglican convent since the Reformation, opened in her parish of Christ Church. As a result, Rossetti underwent a religious crisis in the mid 1850s, which manifested itself in the form of devotional literature like "The Convent Threshold." Although she wrote it in 1858, Rossetti chose to include "The Convent Threshold" in *Goblin Market and Other Poems.*

In 1872, Rossetti published a large anthology of nursery rhymes called *Sing-Song.* "Baby Lies So Fast Asleep" deals with infant death - a frequent reality during Rossetti's time. Rossetti's approach to children's literature reflects the method of Victorian child-rearing, complete with scare tactics and didactic fairy tales.

In 1876, Rossetti published "Bird Raptures," which was set to music by British composer Sir Frederic Hymen Cowen. That same year, she published "De Profundis," inspired by a psalm. Over the years, different composers have set Rossetti's poetry to music. Harold Darke composed the carol "Christmastide" using Rossetti's 1885 poem "Love Came Down at Christmas." Additionally, "In the Bleak Midwinter" was published posthumously in 1904, and set to music by Gustav Holst in 1906. Three years later, Harold Darke composed a more complex interpretation of Holst's version that is now common material for classical choirs.

Character List

Narrator

Rossetti wrote many of her poems in first-person narrative, including the bulk of her devotional work. In these instances, it is difficult to separate the poet's voice from the narrator's. In this particular collection of poems, there are three categories of narrator: the narrator who represents Rossetti's own opinions, the occasional narrator, and the narrator who is separate from the poet. The first type of narrator appears in Rossetti's religious writing, while the second appears in her narrative tales.

The narrator who serves as a mouthpiece for the poet herself is often in dialogue with an absent companion or lover, except in "Love Came Down at Christmas," "In the Bleak Midwinter," "Bird Raptures," "De Profundis," and "A Birthday." These poems instead extol the wonders of Christ's love and the beauty of the natural world. "De Profundis" poses questions to a void, while the narrator of "A Birthday" addresses no one in particular.

"Remember," "The Convent Threshold," and "Up-Hill" all have strong narrators who participate in active dialogue with unseen characters. The third category of narrator, as seen in "Goblin Market" and "Maude Clare," only enters the poem to add useful information, but does not control the outcome of the narrative.

The Young Woman ("Death's Chill Between")

The narrator is a grieving woman who is a character separate from Rossetti herself. Her bereavement is compounded by visions of her beloved, whose death she must learn to accept.

The Young Woman's Mother ("Death's Chill Between")

She never speaks in the poem, but Rossetti implies her presence in through the young woman's responses. The mother wants to soothe her daughter's broken heart and put an end her excessive grief.

The Deceased Young Man ("Death's Chill Between")

The young man's ghost returns to haunt his beloved in the form of footfall, a voice, and a knock.

Maude Clare ("Maude Clare")

She is a queen-like beauty with a broken heart. She brazenly disrupts the wedding between her former lover, Thomas, and Nell, the girl he left Maude for. Maude Clare believes that she should have been the bride. She represents the Victorian archetype of the spurned woman whose dangerous and unruly behavior places her outside social standards.

Sir Thomas ("Maude Clare")

Thomas is Nell's bashful and blushing groom. He broke Maude Clare's heart in the past and now cannot stand up to her rebukes.

Thomas' Mother ("Maude Clare")

Thomas's mother tells her son that she and his father experienced a similar situation to the incident with Maude Clare at the wedding.

Nell ("Maude Clare")

Nell looks like a common village maid compared to Maude Clare, but Thomas thinks that Nell is ideal because of her love and devotion.

The Traveler ("Up-Hill")

The narrator is a weary traveler on a difficult road. She asks her guide questions about the journey ahead and ponders her life.

The Guide ("Up-Hill")

The guide is a source of comfort, and answers all of the narrator's questions about resting spots and the journey ahead.

Lizzie ("Goblin Market")

Lizzie represents the Christ figure in this poem because she saves her sister, Laura, from death. Lizzie's heroic feat proves that she is brave and selfless. Lizzie is beautiful and golden-haired as well as prudent and wise.

Laura ("Goblin Market")

Laura is Lizzie's foolish sister who eats the goblin men's forbidden fruit. Lizzie saves her by obtaining the juice from the goblins' fruit.

Goblins ("Goblin Market")

The goblins are demonic creatures who sell tantalizing fruit. They resemble cats, rats, snails, wombats, and other unseemly creatures. They are also violent, and force their wares upon those, like Lizzie, who do not immediately fall into their trap.

Jeanie ("Goblin Market")

Lizzie and Laura's young friend who ate the goblin men's fruit and gradually pined away into nothingness. Lizzie tells Jeanie's story as a cautionary tale to her curious sister, Laura.

Narrator ("The Convent Threshold")

The narrator is contemplating giving her life to God, and struggles with the sins of her past.

The Lover and the Friend ("The Convent Threshold")

The narrator directs her spiritual musings to these two abstract personae.

God ("The Convent Threshold")

At the end of the poem, the narrator gives her life to God.

Mother ("Baby Lies So Fast Asleep")

She is dealing with the death of her infant child and trying to comfort her surviving child.

Younger Child ("Baby Lies So Fast Asleep")

The younger child asks his/her mother about the baby's death.

Major Themes

Tragic love

The Pre-Raphaelite school of thought placed a high aesthetic value on the idea of unattained love, harkening back to medieval notions of courtship. The underlying belief was that unrealized love preserves an unsullied state of purity. A knight would contemplate the virtues of his beloved from afar, with the distance serving to further safeguard her virtue. This distance between the knight and his maiden could be voluntary or forced, but regardless, the boundary is impenetrable. Rossetti uses this trope several times: Maude Clare is separated from Thomas because he marries another woman, while the young woman in "Death's Chill Between" is separated from her beloved because he dies. Longing for an impossible love creates an emotional image that easily lends itself to powerful art.

Gender and Sexuality

The themes of gender and sexuality feature most prominently in "Goblin Market," but also surface in some degree throughout Rossetti's other work. Although Rossetti did not fully identify with feminism, she recognized the injustice that women faced every day. "Goblin Market" confronts the subject of sexual desire, which was taboo in Victorian England. Laura craves the taste of the fruit, but Lizzie warns her that she will lose her youth and bloom, both euphemisms for her virginity. By the standards of Victorian society, women who engaged in premarital sex were considered "fallen" and therefore, no longer "marriageable." Meanwhile, in the Victorian era, women were just beginning to explore their sexuality, which resulted in challenging society's (read: men's) expectations. Rossetti does not explicitly mention the sexual threats against Lizzie in "Goblin Market." However, Rossetti would have understood the emotional toll of sexual abuse through her work with prostitutes, so the implication is there.

Acceptance of Death

Christina Rossetti's life was plagued with death. Her father died when she was only twenty-four. In addition, tuberculosis was common in the surrounding London homes and infant mortality rates were high. Rossetti's isolated adolescence and zealous devotion to the church led her to spend long periods of time contemplating human mortality. Accepting death is part of the Christian message, especially since Christians believe in the afterlife. In addition to her faith, Rossetti's Pre-Raphaelite companions discouraged material wealth and earthly connections. Rather, Rossetti dwelled on intellectual and religious pursuits, contemplating the soul and the eternal hereafter. Several of her poems reflect her rejection of physical bodies, most notably "Remember," in which she instructs her lover to forget her so that he can be happy.

Renunciation of Desire

Pre-Raphaelite philosophy held that the fulfillment of earthly desire was transient, if not impossible. Instead, the movement encouraged followers to renounce desire altogether, even the desire to live. This belief resulted in melancholy languor and lugubrious contemplation amongst the Pre-Raphaelites. Rossetti believed that the only lasting fulfillment comes from the acceptance of Christ, which will be complete at his Second Coming. She considered any other pursuits, like love, lust, money and fame, to be vain and fruitless.

Divine Love

Divine love is Jesus Christ's love for his people, which Christians believe manifested itself when he was born as a human baby. Divine love is most evident in the nativity and the crucifixion. Rossetti grew up as a devout Anglican and even contemplated becoming a nun. She took religion very seriously and wrote about her existential experiences in depth. Rossetti expounds upon the wonder of divine love in most of her devotional literature, including "Love Came Down at Christmas" and "In the Bleak Midwinter." For Rossetti, divine love gave purpose to her existence and a reason to continue living. Rossetti refers to the crucifixion, which illustrates Christ's unconditional sacrifice, in "Goblin Market."

The Sublime

"The sublime" refers to any natural occurrence that cannot be explained. Throughout her poetry, Rossetti makes allusions to the natural world, which reveals her fascination with the sublime. Great Romantic writers, such as Keats, were also preoccupied with the idea of the sublime. Rossetti's poem "Bird Raptures" resembles Keats' poem about a nightingale on a beautiful night. For Rossetti, the wonders of the natural world are evidence of God's glory. In "A Birthday," Rossetti compares her heart to natural phenomena in order to express her joy at the coming of her beloved Christ.

Religious Doubt

Although Rossetti was devoted to her Anglican faith throughout her lifetime, she questioned her beliefs from time to time. In the 1850s, she suffered a religious crisis, which provided the material for her later devotional poems. "The Convent Threshold" and "De Profundis" question the placement of the universe and Rossetti's purpose within it. Doubt was a normal part of Rossetti's thought process, and guided her spiritual pursuits as well as her writing.

Glossary of Terms

aureole
a circle of light surrounding something, usually in the context of sacred art

beck
a mountain stream

bower
a pleasant shaded place in a garden or a wood

cherubim and seraphim
angels

clad
dressed

clomb
archaic past participle of climb

cloven
split in two

cloy
to sicken with an excess of sweetness

dais
seat of honor or throne

demur
to raise doubts or show reluctance

drouth
poetic form of drought

fickle
changing frequently

fleurs-de-lys
a stylized lily; former royal arms of France

furze
evergreen shrub

girt
fastened

glen
a narrow valley

halcyon
calm, peaceful

hoary
grayish white

hodden
a coarse, woolen cloth

incarnate
embodied in human form

lark
small songbird

lave
to wash

livid
dark bluish gray color; furiously angry

loth
reluctant, unwilling

mien
a person's look or manner

nigh
near

obstreperously
in a disruptive and boisterous manner

paltry
small or meager

pate
a person's head

pellucid
clear

pinion
outer part of a bird's wing, including flight feathers

purloin
to steal something

slake
to satisfy (thirst)

tarry
to delay

vair
bluish-gray squirrel fur

wane
to grow smaller

warble
to sing like a bird

weft
in weaving, the crosswise threads on a loom

Short Summary

This ClassicNote focuses on twelve of Christina Rossetti's poems that represent a variety of styles and phases in her career. These works span her entire professional life, and include sonnets, narrative poems, devotional literature, and folk tale ballads. Rossetti's style was heavily influenced by the Pre-Raphaelite Movement in the visual arts, which was based on close examination, nature, word-painting, and medieval influences.

Rossetti's first published poem, "Death's Chill Between" (1848), marked the dawn of her public career, but she had been writing since childhood. Although this poem feels raw and immature in places, Rossetti portrays strength of feeling and a literary talent that are indicators of her bright future. In this poem, Rossetti expresses the theme of tragic love by focusing on a grieving young woman who must come to terms with her lover's death. Rossetti's next published poem echoed the theme of unrealized passion, but in a different form.

"Maude Clare" (1859) is one of Rossetti's most renowned ballads. It tells the tale of a regal woman whose former lover, Sir Thomas, has married another girl, Nell. Just the newlyweds are leaving the church, Maude Clare accosts them with the details of her affair with Sir Thomas. Maude Clare embodies the Victorian archetype of a scorned woman who is rejected by society because she has failed to meet the expectation of getting married and having a family.

Rossetti also wrote contemplative poems, such as "Up-hill" (1861). This poem is composed of a dialogue between a traveler and a guide about the journey of life and its hardships. The traveler asks about the road ahead, which could either refer to the symbolic journey of life, the transition from life to death, or purgatory.

"Remember" (1862) is a classic Petrarchan sonnet that deals with the acceptance of death. It starts with the narrator asking her lover to remember her when she dies. By the end of the poem, though, she has rescinded her request. This arc represents the Pre-Raphaelite notion of renouncing desire. Rossetti wrote other poems addressing the acceptance of death, including "Baby Lies So Fast Asleep" (1872), which is about infant death.

Rossetti wrote devotional poems as well, including "A Birthday" (1861), "The Convent Threshold" (1862), "De Profundis" (1876), "Love Came Down at Christmas" (1885), and "In the Bleak Midwinter" (1904). The latter two poems celebrate the glory of God's love at Christmas time. In "De Profundis," Rossetti questions the structure of the universe and expresses her desire to escape from her human form. "A Birthday" expresses deep joy about a beloved's birthday, which most likely refers to the Second Coming of Christ. In the "Convent Threshold," Rossetti indicates her devotion to God though the narrator, who dedicates her life to the church.

Rossetti's most famous piece is a narrative poem titled "Goblin Market" (1862). The poem tells the story of two sisters, Lizzie and Laura, who encounter goblin men selling luscious fruit. Lizzie refers to the cautionary tale of their friend Jeanie, who ate the fruit and then died because she could not have any more. However, Laura gives into temptation, tastes the fruit, and becomes dangerously ill as a result. Lizzie returns to the goblins to buy more fruit to cure Laura, but the goblins will not let her have any. Instead, they force fruit on her mouth, but Lizzie manages not to drink its juice. However, the juice is all over her face when she returns to Laura, who consumes the nectar and is cured. Both women live to tell the tale to their children, saying "There is no friend like a sister." There are two interpretations of this poem, both of which are accepted in academic circles. One school of thought is that the sisters' experience represents the Christian redemption of the sinner and the other focuses on the poem's implications about gender and sexuality. In both versions, Lizzie is the savior.

Quotes and Analysis

"For I am bound with fleshly bands,

Joy, beauty, lie beyond my scope;"

"De Profundis" : Lines 13-14

These two lines appear at the beginning of the last stanza of "De Profundis." They are especially important because they represent Rossetti contemplating her mortal state and the resulting limitations. The poet cannot escape her physical being and laments that she is "bound," like a prisoner, constrained by the very flesh that makes her human in the first place. These two lines encapsulate Rossetti's spiritual dilemma. She feels is drawn to sublime beauty which, as a human, she can never possess. However, the paradox lies in the fact that unattainability is what makes this joy and beauty so desirable; it is unsullied.

"Shall I find comfort, travel-sore and weak?

Of labour you shall find the sum.

Will there be beds for me and all who seek?

Yes, beds for all who come."

"Up-Hill": Lines 13-16

This verse concludes Rossetti's poem "Up-Hill," in which she conveys the hardships that devout Christians face during their time on Earth in order to attain certain rewards in the afterlife. This verse mirrors the same pattern as the rest of the poem, as it is structured as a question succeeded by an answer, and then another question followed by another answer to that question. This verse contains the image of a weary traveler receiving just wages for his labor, a common theme in Christianity. Additionally, a resting place is available for anyone who is willing to make the journey, and this sense of repose is aided by the poem's iambic pentameter as well as the gently monosyllabic phrasing of the last two lines.

"Snow had fallen, snow on snow, snow on snow,

In the bleak midwinter, long ago."

"In the Bleak Midwinter": Lines 3-4

These two lines appear at the end of the first verse of "In the Bleak Midwinter." The poet describes a winter scene in the opening verse, and the line "Snow had fallen, snow on snow, snow on snow" adds to the wintry imagery. The repetition of "snow," and "snow on snow, snow on snow" creates musicality and emphasizes the idea that this poem should be recited as lovingly as a nursery rhyme. By repeating the opening line, "In the bleak midwinter," Rossetti attempts to entrance her reader. The phrase "long ago" presents the idea that this is a fable, or an age-old tale.

"Better by far you should forget and smile

Than that you should remember and be sad."

"Remember": Lines 13-14

Typically, the last two lines of a sonnet deliver a short, condensed, and often surprising message, and this poem follows this tradition. The last two lines of Christina Rossetti's sonnet "Remember" emphasize that the narrator is trapped in a paradox. She has spent most of the poem commanding her lover to remember her after she is gone. At the end, by telling her lover to forget her, the narrator abdicates any claim to her lover and therefore, denies herself the fulfillment of her desires, a common theme in Rossetti's poetry.

"My lily feet are soiled with mud,

With scarlet mud that tells a tale

Of hope that was, of guilt that was,

Of love that shall not yet avail;

Alas, my heart if I could bare

My heart, this selfsame stain is there:

I seek the sea of glass and fire

To wash the spot, to burn the snare:

Lo, stairs are meant to lift us higher -

Mount with me, mount the kindled stair."

"The Convent Threshold": Lines 7-16

This segment of the first stanza of "The Convent Threshold" contains intense imagery that symbolizes hope and guilt, both of which are core tenets of Christianity. The lily is a symbol of Christ's purity. The addition of mud shows that the narrator made her journey on foot. The fact that the mud is scarlet suggests that the journey was painful and caused the narrator to bleed. The narrator then acknowledges that objects can tell stories. However, the speaker adds that the story contains "love that shall not yet avail," an idea that suggests the narrator's struggle to accept her promised redemption, as well as her disappointment that this promise is not fulfilled. Her desire to wash off the stain of her sin in a "sea of glass and fire" suggests that she knows that she has not yet finished evolving. Through the image of stairs, the narrator expresses her desire to climb above her existence as an ordinary, sinful human.

"Laura strech'd her gleaming neck -

Like a rush-imbedded swan,

Like a lily from the beck,

Like a moonlit poplar branch,

Like a vessel at the launch

When its last restraint is gone."

"Goblin Market" : Stanza 20

This excerpt from "Goblin Market" marks a turning point for Laura. She is tempted by the fruit that the goblin men are advertising. Rossetti uses a string of nature-based similes to describe Laura's desire. Laura stretches her gleaming neck, one of her most vulnerable body parts, which Rossetti compares to a swan, a lily, or a branch. These objects all have two things in common: they are naturally beautiful, and naturally stuck in a certain position. Rossetti questions Laura's free will and her ability to make moral choices. The comparison of Laura to a vessel, or ship, at a launch, implies her virginity and the fact that her purity will face many threats.

"She cried 'Laura' up the garden,

'Did you miss me?

Come and kiss me.

Never mind my bruises,

Hug me, kiss me, suck my juices

Squeez'd from goblin fruits for you,

Goblin pulp and goblin dew.

Eat me, drink me, love me;

Laura, make much of me;

For your sake I have braved the glen

And had to do with goblin merchant men.'"

"Goblin Market": Stanza 23

This section of "Goblin Market" occurs after Lizzie saves her sister by allowing the goblin men to violate and abuse her instead. After suffering violence at the goblins' hands, Lizzie invites her sister to shower her with excessive, unrestrained affection to receive the juice that is splattered all over her. The rhyme scheme, beginning with "Did you miss me?" follows a simple AABBCC, etc. pattern. This simplicity of the rhyme scheme in Lizzie's speech echoes her earnestness and her heartfelt love for her sister. Her command to "eat me, drink me" is an allusion to Christ. In the ritual of Eucharist, Christians symbolically eat and drink the body of Christ. In this way, Lizzie is the Christ figure in the poem and Laura is the flawed, sinful mortal.

"My heart is like a singing bird

Whose nest is in a water'd shoot;

My heart is like an apple-tree

Whose boughs are bent with thickset fruit;

My heart is like a rainbow shell

That paddles in a halcyon sea;

My heart is gladder than all these

Because my love is come to me."

"Birthday" : Lines 1-8

The first half of "Birthday" follows a pattern in which the narrator compares her heart to images from nature. The repetition of "My heart is like" is representative of the clarity and sincerity that is common in Rossetti's work. The lush images she uses in her similes reflect the influence of Pre-Raphaelite art on her poetry. Each of her chosen images contains a playful combination of movement and rest. For example, the bird is singing but also has its nest, where it can rest. The apple-tree is static, but its heavy fruit is weighing down its boughs. The rainbow shell is inanimate, yet it paddles. However, Rossetti only describes the sea as "halcyon," or extremely calm. Each of these images encompasses a sense of completeness. The singing bird will always come back to its nest; the apple-tree is fulfilled only when the apples weigh down its boughs. Therefore, the narrator's heart is only complete when his or her love is present.

"Baby lies so fast asleep

That no pain can grieve her;

Put a snowdrop in her hand,

Kiss her once and leave her."

"Baby Lies So Fast Asleep", Lines 5-8

The second half of "Baby Lies So Fast Asleep" conveys the message that accepting death is a natural part of life, which is a recurring theme in Rossetti's work. The repetition of the opening line, "Baby Lies So Fast Asleep" creates a sense of comfort and unease simultaneously. The brevity of the poem reflects the brevity of the baby's life. The snowdrop is an important symbol, because it is white and pure like the baby. The word snowdrop can also refer to a short-lived flower that blooms for a few weeks at the end of winter, which mirrors the baby's pure, brief life.

"O herald skylark, stay they flight

One moment, for a nightingale

Floods us with sorrow and delight."

"Bird Raptures", Lines 9-11

In these lines from "Bird Raptures," the narrator commands the skylark to wait until morning to sing so that the nightingale can be heard at night. The nightingale's song is sublimely beautiful, flooding "us with sorrow and delight". This is the only instance in the poem where Rossetti uses the word "us," and it is unclear to whom she is referring. She only asks the skylark to wait "one moment" because she knows the night cannot last, which reflects Rossetti's belief in the transient nature of all things.

Summary and Analysis of "Death's Chill Between" (1848)

Summary:

A young woman nurses her broken heart after the death of her lover. While the woman's mother attempts to pull her daughter out of misery, the young woman wishes either for her beloved to return or for her own death. The narrator asks her mother to let her mourn alone, promising that soon, she will learn how to handle her grief, although death is still welcome. Suddenly, the girl goes into a trance-like state and hears a low voice, soft footfall, and a knock on her door. She believes that her lover has returned, welcomes the deceased young man into the house, and provides refreshments. The young woman promises to protect her beloved from all harm. She says that they will take rest from the sorrow and sing sweet songs together. Talking about weeping jerks the young woman back to reality and her aching heart. She tells her mother that she finally understands that the deceased young man will never return.

Analysis:

"Death's Chill Between" is made up of seven six-line stanzas, each with the rhyme scheme ABABCC and varying between seven and eight syllables in a line. The absence of a strict meter and syllable count make it feel like an elegy, the free flowing grief of a young girl in mourning.

Rossetti crafts a one-sided conversation between a mother and her daughter, who must come to terms with the death of her beloved. The theme of tragic love was a central focus in the ideology of the Pre-Raphaelite movement. The intensity of the young woman's passion matches the acuteness of her grief. Over the course of the poem, she must repress both of these raw emotions and stow them into the recesses of her memory. Her memory is the only place that true love can exist in its unadulterated form, unsullied by the struggles of earthly life. This is a difficult lesson for her to learn, but Pre-Raphaelite philosophy emphasizes the transience of contentment. This defeatist attitude cultivates a lugubrious tone, which is common in Rossetti's work.

Pre-Raphaelite notions of love are similar to medieval representations of courtship. Both of these viewpoints, then, are rooted in Christ's perfect love for the church. In this poem, Rossetti expresses the idea that death protects the integrity of love from being sullied by sin or physical complications. The young woman in "Death's Chill Between" is connected to her dead lover by a "love-cord" rather than a "life-cord," meaning that the connection of love is powerful than life itself. This Gothic-inspired image expresses Rossetti's belief in the intense spiritual connection that exists between the hearts of true lovers. The young woman's lover only comes to her as a phantasm borne from her memory, and not as a physical man. She addresses the deceased young man in apostrophe, not actuality. His soft voice does not call her not into sinful temptation, but rather, ignites the communion of their minds. In this way, their courtly love can only remain pristine in absentia, an ideal that the Pre-Raphaelites embraced.

The Pre-Raphaelites certainly considered spiritual love to be far more meaningful than a physical relationship, but the movement also acknowledged many kinds of love. This poem, for instance, also celebrates the relationship between the grieving daughter and her caring, concerned mother. In turn, the young woman acts maternally towards her lover's ghost. She promises to shelter him from harm and sing him to sleep, like a mother would do for her baby. Although this behavior might seem unusual for two lovers, it shows that the movement's ideals pervade all of the loving relationships in Rossetti's work, not just the romantic ones.

The ideal of tragic love in this poem comes out of the Pre-Raphaelite belief that humans must renounce any and all desire for carnal fulfillment during their existence on earth. That renunciation includes the very desire to remain alive. In the first and third stanza, Rossetti repeats the end rhyme in her narrator's promise to bear her grief. The young woman resolves to be strong in life, although she will "not struggle long". Her preoccupation with her dead lover combined with her resigned attitude towards life suggest that she would welcome her own death. Her renunciation of worldly attachment aligns with Rossetti's religious beliefs as well as her artistic inclinations. Rossetti often expressed the idea that the realms of the mind and spirit transcend the physical world.

Summary and Analysis of "Maude Clare" (1859)

Summary:

Maude Clare interrupts Sir Thomas and Nell's wedding day. She is Sir Thomas' ex-lover and intends to cause trouble for him and the woman he ended up choosing to marry. Maude Clare is regal and makes Nell look like a peasant in contrast. To quell the chaos, Sir Thomas' mother tells her son that she and Thomas' father once found themselves in a similar predicament. She means to comfort Thomas with this information, but instead, Sir Thomas and Nell's faces become worryingly pale. Maude Clare, meanwhile, gives the couple some wedding gifts, all of which are souvenirs from her love affair with Sir Thomas. She gives them her half of a golden chain that Sir Thomas wore when they were together, as well as dried leaves that they jointly picked. Sir Thomas ends up being too embarrassed to rebuff Maude Clare, and so Maude Clare presents her final gift to Nell. She gives the bride permission to accept what remains of Thomas' fickle heart. Nell defiantly declares that she loves Thomas for better and worse and one day, he will love her best.

Analysis:

Rossetti wrote "Maude Clare" in the form of a ballad. It is composed of a dozen four-line stanzas, each with alternating iambic tetrameter and trimeter lines. The rhyme scheme, ABCB, differs from traditional ballads, which are ABAB. The poem consists mainly of dialogue between the characters. The mother speaks to her son, the jilted woman confronts her lover, he responds blusteringly, and the bride defies her romantic predecessor. All of these conversations serve the purpose of shattering the image of marriage as a state of fulfilled love.

Rossetti uses the more spontaneous ABCB rhyme scheme to provide some relief from the strict regularity of the meter. As a result, the meter is awkward at times, paralleling the uncomfortable situation in which the characters are torn between expressing their true emotions and maintaining proper social behavior. The constant battle between restraint and free expression is a recurring theme throughout the piece.

In addition to the contrasting meter and rhyme scheme, Rossetti uses caesurae in Sir Thomas' speech to illustrate his struggle with his emotions. He falters to find an appropriate term of address for his former lover, alternating between the more remote "lady" and "Maude Clare," which belies the close relationship they once shared. Thomas may well be in an awkward situation, but as a man, society will not punish him for his role in it. However, Maude Clare will end up an eternal outcast because she is a woman who defies the societal expectations for her gender.

Maude Clare's aggressive tirade against Thomas and Nell begins with an attention grabbing "lo," and does not soften with her presentation of wedding gifts. She embodies the Victorian archetype of a scorned woman whose wrath cannot be assuaged. Maude Clare's hellcat ire makes Sir Thomas look weak in comparison. However, Maude Clare is the victim in this conflict, albeit unwillingly. She compromised her virtue when she spent intimate moments with Sir Thomas, barefoot in the lily field. In Victorian culture, this level of familiarity outside of marriage detracted from the woman's worth, but not the man's. Marriage formed the structure of a stable society and women who ignored these expectations were considered liminal and dangerous to social harmony. Maude Clare is almost monstrous in her anger, like a savage Juno, but yet, she is a victim of society's conventions.

Nell presents a stark contrast to the unwieldy and aggressively unfeminine Maude Clare. Nell is a loving bride, a paragon of womanly virtue, although she is less stately than her predecessor. Nell also admits that she is less wise and fair than Maude. However, Nell possesses certain attributes that, as a Victorian woman, are worth more than sophistication or status. Nell represents the wholesome goodness of the earth. Her love will sustain Thomas through good times and bad in a way that Maude's never could. Rossetti's comparison of the simple country maid to the stunning femme fatale reveals this inherent contrast.

"Maude Clare," however, is not proof that Rossetti preferred the Victorian ideal of woman to the fiery Maude Clare- types. Rather, Rossetti simply uses this form to comment on the difference between a woman's actual desires and the limitations of her place in Victorian society.

Summary and Analysis of "Up-hill" (1861)

Summary:

Over the course of a journey, the narrator asks her guide eight questions about the road ahead. The narrator asks if the roads are all up-hill and if the journey will take all day. The guide replies in the affirmative. Next, the narrator asks if there is a place to rest for the night and if the darkness will obscure said resting-place from their view. The guide assures the narrator that there is an inn and they will not be able to miss it. The narrator's fifth question is about which other travelers will be on the road. At the inn, the narrator asks if the other travelers would prefer for her to knock or call out. The guide tells the narrator that someone will open the door. Lastly, the narrator asks if there will be a bed for her. The guide tells her that there are beds for everyone.

Analysis:

The question and answer form is common in devotional writing, because it encourages the reader to contemplate his or her own response to the question. The guide addresses the narrator as “my friend," which is also what Christ called his disciples. The poem is comprised of four stanzas with four lines each, following the ABAB rhyme scheme. In this way, the rhyme scheme separates the traveler from the guide, and the simplicity alleviates the pressure of the difficult topic. The meter starts with a trochee and shifts into alternating iambic pentameter and trimeter. The pace is consistent, just like the narrator's steady up-hill climb.

The journey is the prominent symbol in this poem, and is open to a few different interpretations. The first interpretation is that the poem symbolizes the journey from birth to death. The darkening sky foreshadows the end of life, and the inn represents the final resting place. Considering Rossetti's religious background, this final resting place could be interpreted as Heaven. The act of knocking on the door represents the Christian confession of sin and the need for forgiveness before admittance into Heaven. When describing this moment, Rossetti chooses to use a nearly verbatim quote from the Gospel of Matthew. Rossetti frames death as a form of respite after the tiring journey of life.

There is a slight possible variation on the interpretation that the road represents the journey of life. Already careworn, the weary traveler wonders if life grows easier as she grows older. However, the guide tells her that the road that remains is up-hill and arduous. This interpretation does not resolve the symbolism behind the inn. It is possible that the inn could represent death, which also provides an opportunity for rest at the end of the road.

A third reading seems less likely because of Rossetti's religious views, but it is worth examining. This school of thought considers the journey to represent Christian purgatory. In this case, the inn would also represent Heaven, just like in the first interpretation. "Up-hill" is a classic example of Rossetti's devotional literature, which dealt with doubt as well as eternal assurance. The road takes on several meanings, each revealing a facet of Rossetti's contemplation of life and its hardships.

Summary and Analysis of "A Birthday" (1861)

Summary:

The narrator of "A Birthday" expresses her delight about her love's upcoming birthday. The narrator, who most likely voices Rossetti's own views, compares her heart to various things in nature. She uses the images of a songbird, a fruit-laden apple-tree, and a rainbow to express the depth of her love. She asks for an elaborate golden throne carved in wood. She joyfully exclaims that the birthday of her love and her life has arrived.

Analysis:

Rossetti divides this sixteen- line poem into two eight-line stanzas, each with an irregular rhyme pattern.

The narrator expresses the fullness of her heart upon the occasion of her love's birthday by starting every comparison in the first stanza with "My is heart is like". Rossetti's use of anaphora, evident in the repetition of this line, emphasizes the narrator's inability to articulate her joy through language. She continues to search for an appropriate simile for her feelings, using symbols that invoke images of celebration and happiness. The laden apple-tree promises the nourishment of fruit. The rainbow signifies God's promise to Noah and mankind that he will not flood the earth again.

Through these similes, the narrator attempts to express her joy about the arrival of her love. This "love" could be a man, but this is unlikely. It is probable that her "love" is somehow connected to her Christian faith. The love could represent Easter and the arrival of Spring, which signals rebirth and rejuvenation. The images in this poem could certainly pertain to the arrival of spring.

Rossetti frequently refers to the Second Coming of Christ as the ultimate "birthday" in her work. The Second Coming is central to the Christian faith, because it symbolizes the new kingdom replacing the old Earth. In her description of the purple throne, Rossetti draws upon the imagery of the Temple of Jerusalem from the Old Testament, which represents God's presence on Earth.

It is clear that regardless of whom the "love" represents, the narrator feels extreme joy at his or her arrival. A singing bird uses melody to express itself similar to the way that humans use words. Similarly, the narrator reveals the longing of her heart with the freedom of a bird. She personifies the other objects, imbuing them with human capabilities and emotions. This connection between nature and the divine common amongst Pre-Raphaelite poets and artists.

Analysis:

Summary and Analysis of "Goblin Market" (1862)

Summary:

Every evening, when sisters Lizzie and Laura go to fetch water from a nearby stream, they must listen to the tempting calls of goblin men selling delicious fruit. Lizzie fears the goblins and admonishes her sister to do the same. When they catch sight of the goblins displaying their wares on golden platters, Lizzie runs home, but Laura is entranced. Despite the goblins' demonic appearance, resembling cats, rats, snails and covered in whiskers, Laura hears only the coo of doves. The goblins see her and repeat their cry. Although Laura has no money, the goblins accept a lock of her hair as payment for the fruit. Laura drinks her fill of fruit juice and returns home, intoxicated by the sweet nectars. She brings one fruit stone (pit) home with her.

Lizzie meets Laura at the gateway to their home and scolds her sister for returning late. She recounts the tale of their friend Jeanie, who ate a piece of the goblin fruit and then pined away to her death because she could not get any more. Laura assures her sister that all is well and that she plans to buy enough fruit for both of them the next day. The sisters proceed with their housework. The next day, Laura discovers that she cannot see the goblins anymore nor hear their calls, although Lizzie still can. Laura pines for the fruit, losing her health and youthful vigor. After some futile attempts to plant the fruit pit, Laura despairs. She stops eating and working.

Lizzie fears that Laura will die soon, so she places a silver penny in her purse and goes to the goblin men. She asks for fruit for her sister, but the goblins instead invite Lizzie to join their feast. When she refuses, the goblins beat her and try to force the fruit into her mouth, smearing her face with juice. She does not succumb, and the goblins soon tire of torturing her.

Lizzie returns home and tells Laura to kiss the juice on her face, and Laura does so. The juice acts like a poison and Laura collapses into a deathlike state. Lizzie remains by her sister's side through the night and in the morning, Laura awakens, her health and beauty restored. Years later, when they are both married, the two sisters tell their children the tale of the goblin men. Laura ends the story with the moral, "there is no friend like a sister."

Analysis:

This narrative poem has an irregular rhyme scheme and loose iambic tetrameters, which quickens the pace. The loose meter allows for the narrators' spontaneity, and the rapid pace lends a tone of urgency. Lizzie and Laura, the narrators, deliver the poem as a lesson to their children.

There are two popular interpretations of “Goblin Market”: one reading is religious, and the other focuses on gender and sexuality. Because it is difficult to prove Rossetti's original intent, scholars have invented a useful dichotomy. If the reader is more familiar with the religion, the reader will see the Christian allegory. However, if the reader is well versed in the study of gender and sexuality, then the symbolism will more readily relate to that topic. These interpretations are not mutually exclusive; rather, they should be viewed in tandem to extract the maximum meaning from this poem.

In the Christian interpretation, Laura represents Eve, the goblin men are the equivalent of Satan, their fruit is the temptation to sin, and Lizzie is the Christ figure. Laura sins by going against the interdiction that she must not eat the goblins’ fruit, which is an homage to Adam and Eve eating the forbidden fruit in the Book of Genesis. The long list of the goblins' fruit represents the wide variety of temptations that humans face during their lifetimes. Like Adam and Eve, Laura discovers that the fruit does not bring fulfillment, but rather, death and destruction.

Meanwhile, Lizzie suffers the consequences of Laura’s sin in order to rescue her sister from the punishment of death, just like Christ. The red fruit juice that Lizzie tries to get Laura to drink is like the blood of Christ in the Eucharist. Rossetti describes Lizzie as a pure “lily in a flood," and that is why she is the only person who is able to save Laura’s life. The sacrifice Lizzie makes for her sister comes out of pure love and true friendship.

The second interpretation of "Goblin Market" is based on symbols of repressed sexual desire and sexual violence. Lizzie and Laura are both innocent and virginal at the beginning of the poem, but Laura’s curiosity proves to be stronger than her sister’s warning. Rossetti creates an uncomfortable struggle between the consequences of pursuing lust and the need to explore natural human desires. Amidst charged language like “sucked” and “heaved,” Laura loses her youth and bloom (her virginity, essentially) as a result of taking the goblin men's tempting fruit. In Victorian society, a woman’s deflowering marks her transition into adulthood as a wife and mother. However, because Laura is not married, the encounter strips her of her "maiden" status prematurely. Laura did not heed her sister's warning, and now, just like Jeanie, she will suffer.

Lizzie's trajectory in this interpretation, however, is not quite as straightforward. Rossetti uses the language of sexual violence when the goblin men attack her with fruit, but Lizzie refuses to drink the juice. Meanwhile, she manages to hold onto her virtue in the form of the silver penny, which has a double meaning - "silver penny" was an Elizabethan term for the female genitalia. Lizzie makes a sacrifice so that Laura can heal and recover. However, the difficulty of this interpretation is that lost maidenhood cannot be recovered. Instead, Laura’s redemption could be refer to her reintroduction into normal social relationships, because at the end of the poem, she is married with children.

The motto, “there is no friend like a sister,” coincides with the feminist theme. Sisterhood and female community were important to Rossetti, who worked with prostitutes at the St. Mary Magdalene Home for Fallen Women. Perhaps she hoped that through this poem, even fallen women could seek a path to redemption, leaving their past indiscretions behind. However, there is a darker side to the feminist interpretation. Much of the language in “Goblin Market” refers to buying and selling. In Victorian England, women were expected to follow a certain standard of conduct. Failure to meet these standards led to the depreciation of a woman’s worth when she came to the marriage "market." Unlike Laura, Lizzie heeds the warning and safeguards her money in her purse, thereby protecting her maidenly virtue.

Summary and Analysis of "Remember" (1862)

Summary:

The narrator, who presumably represents Rossetti, addresses her beloved and encourages him to remember her after her death. She asks him to remember her even when his memory of her begins to fade. Eventually, the narrator gives this person (it is unclear if he or she is real or imagined) her permission to forget her gradually because it is better to "forget and smile" than to "remember and be sad."

Analysis:

"Remember" is a Petrarchan sonnet in iambic pentameter, consisting of an ABBA ABBA octave and a CDE CDE sestet.

Rossetti repeats the word "remember" throughout the entire poem, as if the narrator fears that her beloved will not heed her request. Rossetti also uses repetition to underline the vast boundary between life and death, writing "gone away," and later, "gone far away." The "silent land" is a symbol of death, emphasizing the narrator's loneliness without her beloved rather, which is stronger than her fear of death itself. Acceptance of death is common in Pre-Raphaelite philosophy. Pre-Raphaelites believed that material troubles pale in comparison to the struggles of the mind.

The tone of the octave is contemplative and reconciliatory on the topic of death. The narrator can finally be at peace because she has renounced her desire for earthly pleasures, such as the physical presence of her beloved. She is even accepting of death, content to exist only in her beloved's memory. However, she has not yet made peace with the possibility that her lover will forget her; this form of death would be more painful than her physical expiration.

Even though the narrator seems to reach peace with her death at the end of the octave, the Pre-Raphaelite belief system demands a further renunciation of human desire. The narrator's tone changes with the volta, which is the break between the octave and the sestet. The volta typically accompanies a change in attitude, which is true in this poem. The narrator even renounces the need to be remembered, which is ironic because the poem is titled "Remember." She wishes for her beloved to be happy, even if that means forgetting her. The narrator sacrifices her personal desire in an expression of true love.

"Remember" ultimately deals with the struggle between physical existence and the afterlife. Rossetti grapples with the idea of a physical body, which is subject to decay and death, and how it relates to an eternal soul.

Summary and Analysis of "The Convent Threshold" (1862)

Summary:

Christina Rossetti's poem "The Convent Threshold" expresses the struggle between the narrator's doubt and her belief in Christianity. She begins by expounding on the strength of blood relations and then describes the bloody mud on her feet. This mud tells a tale that will unfold in the upcoming lines. On an expository level, the narrative follows a person climbing stairs to rise above her sinful human existence.

Rossetti develops the contrast between one who looks Heaven-ward and one who looks towards Earth. Looking up, the narrator sees a vision of Heaven as a grand city, where the righteous souls sing hymns alongside angels. These righteous beings partake in a feast, which symbolizes the death of Christ and the sacrifices he made for the sins of man. As a result of these beings' righteousness, their faces gleam brighter than the sun. In comparison, the humans down on Earth have milky white faces that have become flushed and healthy with wine. Although the humans on Earth are happy at this moment, the narrator reminds her readers that their living days are running out. She also encourages her reader to engage in acts of spiritual devotion before death comes.

By the fourth stanza, the narrator reminisces that she and whomever she is addressing have both engaged in pleasant sin. However, they now must repent. The narrator wishes that she had not lived her life the "easy way." She believes that joy and love are fleeting, and if one does not repent, he or she will experience long years of regret before death. The human body will not last, the narrator declares to her audience. The narrator then continues exploring the contrast between paradise and Earth, emphasizing that while life may be long and sorrowful, it will end one day. Therefore, it is vital to repent in order to save one's soul and lead it to paradise.

In the seventh stanza, the narrator relates her dream from the night before, in which a figure resembling Lucifer battles for power. After his greedy quest for "light" and knowledge," he falls gruesomely. Rossetti describes him collapsing under the weight of knowledge, and she uses his fall to demonstrate that although knowledge is important, love is sweet and therefore, greater.

After the narrator's disturbing dream, God asks her if she had been dreaming of Him. The narrator attempts to reject this idea. Although she does not mention it explicitly, the narrator's audience in the next few stanzas is likely God or Jesus. After the narrator's attempt to push God away, both parties end up feeling devastated.

In the ninth and final stanza, the narrator alternates between sleep plagued by dreams of God and waking up to pray against her will. The narrator undergoes a religious experience which she cannot describe in words. This intense struggle between doubt and belief eventually alters her appearance: her hair turns gray and her face becomes wrinkled. She wonders if God will ask her what happened to His beloved face. The narrator undergoes a transition when she expresses her earnest desire to be with her beloved God and Jesus Christ in Heaven.

Analysis:

Christina Rossetti's poem "The Convent Threshold" reflects the poet's struggle between her doubt and her belief in Christianity. In the title and the first stanza of the poem, Rossetti makes it apparent that her narrator has not yet fully committed to a life of devotion, but rather, is standing at the threshold (literally meaning "doorway") of doing so. The first stanza contains contains imagery of blood, invoking the sacrificial blood of Christ. Christians believe that Christ's blood can protect human beings from our own sinful nature. In the poem, blood forms the bond between the narrator and her beloved.

The second stanza sets up the contrast between Heaven and Earth. In Rossetti's vision of Heaven, she portrays righteous devotion through the image of a feast. This feast symbolizes the Christian ritual of the Eucharist, or Communion. Meanwhile, she describes the righteous beings' lives on Earth, where they were martyrs: "racked, roasted, crushed, wrenched limb." Here, Rossetti emphasizes the Christian belief that life on Earth can be difficult, but it will pay off in the afterlife as long as a person remains committed to his or her faith.

In contrast to the gleaming faces of the righteous beings in Heaven, the humans living on Earth have milky-white complexions flushed by wine. They sing, fall in love, and are happy. While Rossetti does not negatively judge these humans, she makes sure to warn her audience that death is near and that their happiness will be short-lived unless they repent. The repetition at the end of the third stanza, "Why will you die? Why will you die?" heightens the sense of urgency surrounding the question of human mortality. When she addresses her beloved, the narrator names the parts of his body that will one day disappear, like his cheeks, his eyes, and his hair. At the end of the fifth stanza, she displays a devastated outlook on life through her repetition: "O weary life, O weary Lent, O weary time whose stars are few."

The sixth stanza solidifies the narrator's acceptance that repentance is necessary for salvation, yet her faith becomes shaky after her disturbing dream. She dreams about Lucifer and his minions battling for glory and power in Heaven. The prophet Isaiah tells relates this story in the Old Testament, which forms part of the foundation of Christian theology. Although Rossetti does not explicitly name Lucifer in "The Convent Threshold," there are many obvious clues, like the repeated line "Give me light!" (Lucifer's name means light). Rossetti links light closely with knowledge, and it is possible that she is referring to the European quest for enlightenment through rational thought. Rossetti herself often felt a personal conflict between irrational feelings and rational doubt. However, in this poem, she concludes her description of the dream with the strong assertion that faith is greater than knowledge.

At this point, the narrator's inner struggle with belief is still playing out. It is unclear who comes to the narrator in the dark hours before dawn, but it could be God, Jesus, or perhaps the Holy Spirit. The narrator says that her heart used to get excited by God, but it is now like dust: lifeless, dirty, and showing traces of her worn-down life. Rossetti makes a powerful choice to refer to God as a playfellow or lover who shares the narrator's bed. This image of the relationship between God and His followers was common in medieval literature, which Rossetti grew up with because her father was a scholar of Dante. When the narrator tries to persuade God to leave her, they are both devastated, as if they were star-crossed lovers in an epic tragedy.

In the final stanza, the narrator undergoes more inner turmoil as she wakes from dreaming about "you," which presumably refers to God. She prays against her will, which suggests her physical inability to reject Christianity and God's love. Her gray hair and wrinkled face show that she has gone through an intense religious experience, but also symbolize the transience of human life. In a sense, this is the moment when she crosses the "threshold" to accepting God. After her religious experience, the narrator describes God as "an old familiar love," which echoes the poem's opening statement about how familial ties of blood and love cannot be broken.

Analysis:

Summary and Analysis of "Baby Lies So Fast Asleep" (1872)

Summary:

The narrator is a mother, explaining the death of her baby to her youngest surviving child using a more gentle euphemism: sleep. The child asks if the angels will take the deceased baby to Heaven. The mother tells her child that the baby is asleep and far away from harm. She tells the child to place a flower in the dead baby's hand, kiss the body, and come away.

Analysis:

This poem consists of eight lines that do not rhyme, although Rossetti uses "asleep" as a final word twice and "her" at the end of four lines. The lack of a rhyme scheme creates a solemn atmosphere that is appropriate for the subject matter: a baby's untimely death.

Rossetti uses constant end-stopping that gives the poem a halting quality, as if the mother is too bereaved to speak of her baby's death, even while she is trying to comfort her child about the same reality. The child's question about Heaven introduces the concept of life after death, and it seems from the mother's response that she truly believes that her baby is now in Heaven. However, she still hesitates to relinquish her baby's body to the kindly angels dressed in white, so it is possible that she even does not fully embrace what she is telling her child about the afterlife. She would rather tell her child, and perhaps even herself, that the baby is only sleeping, because it feels less permanent than death.

Rossetti frequently compares sleep to death in her work, and in this case, it is important to consider that in the Victorian era, infant death was as normal as nightly repose. Unfortunately, women had to face infant mortality as a frequent and harsh reality, like the mother in this poem,. There was also a high rate of infanticide, due to the lack of pregnancy prevention methods. To that end, women who killed their children would describe them as "asleep" or "resting" so as to protect themselves from the brutality of their crimes. Although this is a dark topic for a nursery rhyme, the theme of child mortality was a reality during Rossetti's time and frequently occurs in children's poetry collections from the period.

The poem does not end on a completely melancholy note. The mother tells her younger child to put a snowdrop in the baby's hand. Snowdrops are among the first flowers to appear at the onset of spring, and are often poetic symbols of eternal hope. According to a Christian legend, an angel gave Adam and Eve a snowdrop after their expulsion from Eden, just when they were despairing that winter would never end.

This melancholy poem provides insight into the world of Victorian child-rearing practices and the commonplace occurrence of infant death. In this way, Rossetti shows that children had to learn about fragility of life from a very young age.

Summary and Analysis of "Bird Raptures" (1876)

Summary:

"Bird Raptures" praises the sublime beauty of night, epitomized by the nightingale's song. Rossetti asks the moon to rise and wake the nightingale so that the world can hear its "wordless tale." She requests the lark to wait until morning to sing so that she can fully enjoy the nightingale's song.

Analysis:

This poem contains three stanzas of five lines each, with an ABABB CBCBB DBDBB rhyme scheme. The first and third B rhyme of every stanza contains the word "nightingale," emphasizing its importance in the poem. The rhyme scheme also lends the poem a musical quality, almost like the warbling of a bird.

Celebrated poets like Keats and Homer frequently praised the nightingale's melodic song in their work. Poets have continued to use the nightingale's free and unique tune as a symbol of poetic inspiration. On the other hand, the nightingale can also invoke a tone of plaintive lament because of its frequent appearance in mythology as a symbol of death in war.

In this poem, Rossetti uses the nightingale as a symbol for the beauty of night and the natural world. Rossetti extols the virtues of the night instead of celebrating sunlight, which many poets of her time were wont to do. Although night often symbolizes danger and temptation for sin in Christian allegory, Rossetti finds evidence of God's grace in the darkness. Her repetition of the imperative "Make haste" emphasizes the intensity of her desire to commune with the beauty of night.

Rossetti's praise of the sublime is rooted in the Romantic appreciation of inexplicable phenomena in nature. While listening to the beauty of the nightingale, she forgets her earthly worries and is swept up in the beauty of the bird's song.

Summary and Analysis of "De Profundis" (1876)

Summary:

Christina Rossetti begins her poem "De Profundis" by questioning the arrangement of the universe, observing that Earth feels isolated from the stars. The narrator goes on to complain that even the monotonously revolving moon is out of her reach. Whenever she looks at the stars and sun, she has a strong desire to escape her human, Earth-bound state. Although she is aware of the futility of her wish to attain the "joy and beauty" of the universe, she still strains her heart towards the stars and tenuously holds onto the hope that she can reach them.

Analysis:

The poem "De Profundis" deals with the narrator's longing to escape from her mortal existence and attain eternal bliss. The poem begins with an apostrophe, questioning the arrangement of the universe. The structure and word-choice in these opening lines, heaven "built" and earth "set," suggest that the narrator believes in the idea of a creator of the universe, although she does not specify the creator in the poem.

The poem follows an ABAB rhyme scheme. In the second stanza, Rossetti refers to the moon with the pronoun "she," writing that the moon "repeats her tune," and therefore personifies the moon. Additionally, it is possible to interpret the narrator's feminization of the moon as an expression of her affinity to its repetitive, circular existence. Later, the narrator mildly disparages the moon's monotonous cycle, essentially admitting that she would not want to reach it. She does have a contradictory attitude, though, because she also expresses her jealousy of the moon for being so far away.

Additionally, Rossetti expresses the narrator's admiration for the majestic beauty of the stars and sun through constructed poetic devices, which mostly appear in the third stanza. For example, Rossetti adds musicality with the elision in "scatter'd fire" and the consonance within the phrase "far-trailing train." The colon at the end of the third stanza marks a sudden turn in the poem.

The fourth stanza reveals the narrator's acceptance of her human state, even though she illustrates it with the image of a bound prisoner. The parallel structure and alliteration in the line, "I strain my heart, I stretch my hands" suggests the narrator's determination to continue trying to attain the unattainable.

"De Profundis" means "Out of the Deep" and originally refers to Psalm 130 in the Bible, which is an important psalm of repentance in Christian liturgy. This psalm laments the human's miserable wretched state and may have influenced Rossetti when she was writing "De Profundis." Psalm 130 and "De Profundis" also express similar themes of hope and determination.

Summary and Analysis of "Love Came Down at Christmas" (1885)

Summary:

In "Love Came Down at Christmas," Christina Rossetti praises the divine love that, according to the New Testament, humans could only access after the birth of Jesus Christ. With the line, "Love was born at Christmas," Rossetti equates Jesus Christ with Love. She states that this love should be the key to human existence, and people should consider divine love as the essential quality of being.

Analysis:

"Love came down at Christmas" is made up of three stanzas with four lines each. The first two stanzas follow an ABCB pattern and the final stanza follows a DBDB pattern. The lyrics are simple and sincere, which lends heartfelt feeling to the poem. Composers have since set the words to music, transforming Rossetti's piece into a popular Christmas carol.

The theme of the poem is evident through Rossetti's repeated use of the word "love." She starts eight lines with "love." Her use of anaphora emphasizes the idea that Christ was born as a human so that he could share his divine love with mankind.

Rossetti invokes the narrative surrounding Christ's birth without using specific details. For this reason, the poem might feel cryptic to readers who are unfamiliar with the Bible. "Love came down at Christmas" refers to Jesus Christ's birth unto the Virgin Mary. Shepherds who were tending their flocks and three wise kings in a distant land saw David's star in the sky and took it as a divine sign. The shepherds came immediately to witness the incarnation of Christ as man in the form of the baby Jesus. Rossetti describes Christ's love as "love incarnate, love divine."

In the last stanza of the poem, Rossetti calls for love and fellowship amongst her Christian brothers and sisters. She believed that Christ's love was the essential facet of her religion.

Summary and Analysis of "In the Bleak Midwinter" (1904)

Summary:

In "In the Bleak Midwinter," Rossetti begins her poetic retelling of the Nativity story by describing attributes of the winter season, which is when Christians celebrate the birth of Jesus Christ. In this scene, there are traditional elements of the traditional Nativity story found in gospels of the New Testament, including the stable where Jesus was born, his mother, the Virgin Mary, and the angels and animals who worshipped the baby. Rossetti concludes by imagining herself in the position of a Shepherd and Wise Man, and declares that her heart is the one gift she can offer Jesus.

Analysis:

Rossetti opens "In the Bleak Midwinter" with a simple yet powerful description of winter. Her personification of the moaning wind gives the first line a child-like tone. Rossetti pairs up natural elements for straightforward similes: "Earth stood hard as iron, water like a stone." The simple couplet rhyme scheme, which continues throughout the poem, gives the reader a sense that Rossetti is telling a familiar and much beloved tale. The phrase "Long ago" adds to the nursery-tale tone.

Rossetti does not introduce Christ and his human incarnation until after the first stanza. When she finally does, it clearly becomes the focal point of the poem. The second stanza encompasses the core of Christian theology: Christ must be born on earth, live and die as a human, and then be resurrected and return at the end of the Earth. In the midst of this complex theology, Rossetti includes the repetition of her opening line, "In the bleak midwinter," as if to bring comfort to such mysterious and detached theological doctrine.

The third stanza shows Jesus as content with the lowly circumstances of his birth. Rossetti's word choice is appropriately humble, as she repeats the pattern, "Enough for Him, whom..." in the first and third lines of this stanza.

In the fourth verse, Rossetti contrasts the magnificent divine with the humble circumstances of Jesus' nativity. She borrows the biblical phrases "Angels and archangels" and "cherubim and seraphim," allowing the internal rhyme sounds to enhance the poem's melodic meter. She emphasizes the importance of Christ's humanity through the image of Christ's mother kissing her baby. In this verse, Rossetti also celebrates the unique value of human love.

In the fifth and final stanza, the poet places herself in the poem by wondering what gift she would offer the baby Jesus if given the chance. Her repetition of "If I were" and "what can I give Him" in this stanza add to the child-like earnestness of the poem. In general, Rossetti limits her poetic devices to the song-like aa bb couplet rhyme scheme. However, her restraint speaks volumes about her attitude towards divine mysteries that require a child's innocent and sincere faith. The final enjambment in the last line suggests the poet's decisiveness in her desire to give her heart to Jesus.

Suggested Essay Questions

1. **Compare and contrast the tragic love in "Maude Clare" and "Death's Chill Between." Why is the young woman an unsympathetic character? How could the inclusion of the additional stanzas (that Rossetti actually wrote) change the reader's view of Maude Clare?**

   Both of these poems center around unrealized love. Although Sir Thomas does not return Maude Clare's love, the reader feels a sense of embarrassment and pity for her outburst. The problem is that the poem does not contain much information about Maude Clare and Sir Thomas' emotional relationship and subsequently, her motivations to confront her former lover. Rossetti had written additional stanzas explaining Maude Clare's character more thoroughly, which soften the tone of her attack on the married couple. As the poem stands, though, Maude Clare comes off as the aggressor because of her strong will. By contrast, the young woman in "Death's Chill Between" does read as a victim because she reacts to the death of her lover with ladylike sadness, instead of ferocious anger.
2. **How does Rossetti juxtapose the nightingale and the skylark in "Bird Raptures"? What does this contrast demonstrate about her views on natural beauty?**

   In the poem, Rossetti shows more appreciation for the nightingale, who comes out at night, than the lark, who sings during daytime hours. Rossetti prefers the nightingale because it is rare to hear its song, which makes it more special for Rossetti and her companion. The song of the nightingale is transient, unlike the lark's call, which is much more common. Therefore, the nightingale's song is elevated to sublime status. Rossetti's preference for nighttime and the nightingale illustrates her fascination with sublime beauty which, by definition, is not accessible or commonplace.
3. **Discuss the crisis of faith after the narrator's dream in "The Convent Threshold," and explore why Rossetti may have chosen to write about a dream in this instance.**

   The dream of Lucifer, who was determined to acquire "light" and knowledge, serves as a warning to the narrator not to blindly pursue these things. Rossetti often invokes a dream state to offer a glimpse into a character's true desire, and subsequently, reveal an innate crisis of humanity. Here, Rossetti uses the dreamscape to contrast irrational love and rational knowledge, both of which are important to the Christian faith. However, an unquestioning love of God is the most vital tenet of the religion, according to Rossetti.
4. **In "Love Came Down at Christmas," Rossetti sets the stage for the nativity story by describing a familiar winter scene. Discuss her use of poetic devices in the juxtaposition of the humble and the magnificent.**

Rossetti uses couplets to foreshadow the entry of the carpenter king, who was both lowly and exalted. At first, couplets appear to be simple and ordinary. However, in this instance, Rossetti's couplets complete each other, fulfilling the first word with a new word. Jesus, as the second Adam, filled an empty place. Additionally, the narrator of Christ's birth story is poor, but Rossetti still makes sure to include him in this tale of divine magnificence.

5. **Describe Rossetti's use of the sonnet form in "Remember." Identify the turning points in the poem and discuss whether or not the sonnet form relates to the message.**

   Rossetti uses the form of the Petrarchan sonnet to illustrate the mental process of her narrator, who is contemplating the value of being remembered. In the beginning octave, the narrator asks her lover to remember her even though she cannot be with him. The narrator makes a dramatic turn with the volta between the stanzas. In the last sestet, the narrator renounces her need to be remembered.

6. **Discuss the various meanings of the journey in "Up-hill". What are the possible interpretations of "journey"?**

   In "Up-hill," the journey could represent one of three things: the narrator's road towards death, her journey of life, or her crossing into the afterlife. All of these interpretations, however, are thematically similar - expressing the difficulty of life on Earth and the uncertainty of what happens after death. It is also possible that Rossetti used "journey" as a metaphor to describe the writing process, with the inn representing the final written piece.

7. **How does Rossetti treat the matter of free will or agency in "Goblin Market"?**

   Rossetti's version of the fall of man embodies the standard Christian beliefs about human free will. Laura knows that she should not eat the goblins' fruit, but she chooses to do so anyway. Lizzie warns her sister not to take the risk, but ultimately knows that the decision belongs to Laura. After Laura exerts her powers of agency, she is subsequently trapped by her choice. She can no longer live a normal life after tasting the goblins' fruit. At the end of the poem, Lizzie jumps into action and saves Laura. This trajectory corresponds to Christian notions of choice, slavery to sin, and the freedom to act.

8. **In the poem "A Birthday," Rossetti uses several poetic devices to express her joy at the arrival of her beloved. Explain the effectiveness of these devices in enhancing the poem's emotional impact.**

   Rossetti's narrator compares her heart to a series of phenomena that occur in the natural world, including a fruit-laden tree, a young plant, a rainbow, and a songbird. This repetition of similes gives the lines an air of excitement, building up the reader's anticipation about what the narrator will feel when she finally meets her love face-to-face. By the end of the poem, the most resonant moment is the narrator's admission that she cannot find the right words to express what she is feeling. In this way, Rossetti uses the limitations of language as a device to increase the power of the reader's emotional experience.

9. **Choose a classic interpretation of "Goblin Market" - either from a feminist, Christian, or moral/social perspective, and discuss the merits and/or flaws of that interpretation.**

   The feminist interpretation of "Goblin Market" focuses on the charged imagery of ripe fruit, the threats of male sexuality and Rossetti's frank inclusion of female desire. This interpretation, however, is problematic because in Victorian times, Laura would have never been able to return to her youth and beauty after losing her virtue. Additionally, Lizzie is the victim of sexual violence when she goes to save Laura, but somehow, Lizzie's virtue is not tainted. In the Christian interpretation, Laura represents Eve, the goblin men are the equivalent of Satan, their fruit is the temptation to sin, and Lizzie is the Christ figure.

10. **What does the narrator in "De Profundis" believe about beauty and joy? How does this align with Rossetti's Pre-Raphaelite beliefs?**

    The narrator implies that sublime phenomena represents beauty that can only be seen from a distance. The "scattered fire" of stars and the "sun's far-trailing train" are sublime images that only appear beautiful when seen from afar. This idea is inspired by the Pre-Raphaelite doctrine that love at its purest can only exist when the lovers are separated. Similarly, during this narrator's life on Earth, she must be satisfied with longing for the moon, but never being able to touch it.

The Pre-Raphaelite Movement

In 1848, William Holman Hurt, John Everett Millais, and Dante Gabriel Rossetti founded the "Pre-Raphaelite Brotherhood" in order to unite English painters, poets, and critics who wanted to reform English art. According the three founders, the quality of art had deteriorated during the High Renaissance, because Raphael, Michelangelo, and their contemporaries favored highly stylized poses and artificial compositions over the intense realism, natural influence, and jewel-like brilliance of Quattrocento Italian Art.

Additionally, the members of the Brotherhood felt that the Royal Academy of Art, under the leadership of Sir Joshua Reynolds, was undermining the academic study of painting by promoting these lax and "sloshy" techniques. The Brotherhood was based in London and eventually grew to seven members with the addition of William Michael Rossetti, James Collinson, Frederic George Stephens, and Thomas Woolner. They promoted their ideas by writing and publishing a newspaper called *The Germ.*

The Pre-Raphaelite Brotherhood was not dogmatic, but they did define their doctrines. They declared that Pre-Raphaelite artists must:

1) Have genuine ideas to express,

2) Study nature attentively, so as to know how to express it,

3) Sympathize with what is direct and serious and heartfelt in previous art, to the exclusion of what is conventional and self-parodying and learned by rote.

4) Most indispensable of all, to produce thoroughly good pictures and statues.

Although the Pre-Raphaelite Movement was primarily centered around the visual arts, Christina Rossetti's poetry belongs to the literary branch of the Pre-Raphaelite aesthetic. Her brother, Dante Gabriel Rossetti, illustrated some of her poems in the Pre-Raphaelite style, including "Goblin Market." Additionally, Christina modeled for her brother's painting "The Girlhood of the Virgin Mary," which was one of the first paintings to bear the signature "PRB" - the Brotherhood's hallmark.

Influenced by her brother's leadership in the Pre-Raphaelite Brotherhood, Christina Rossetti's poetry adheres to the ideals of the movement. While abundantly rich in detail, her poetry strives for clarity in meaning through its relatively simple rhyme schemes and language. Like the Pre-Raphaelites, she draws from literary sources of the past.

Also present in Rossetti's poetry is the Pre-Raphaelite obsession with symbols. Rossetti practices word-painting in her poetry, where a word or combination of words can conjure up a strong, clear image. She draws her use of symbols from the medieval period, during which which tokens and blazons were common in both art and literature. Ultimately, the Pre-Raphaelite Movement was a precursor to the European movement of Symbolism, which emerged in the late 19th century and blossomed in the early 20th century.

During the growth of the Pre-Raphaelite Brotherhood, a schism formed between those who favored medievalism and those who embraced realism. Originally, Dante Gabriel Rossetti and his followers emulated the medieval period, because of its unique creative energy and innovation. In addition, the original Pre-Raphaelites drew inspiration from the medieval period, when the predominant belief was that art was a spiritual, not a material, endeavor. Christina Rossetti took her brother's side, and her poetry is steeped in Anglo-Catholic beliefs. Poems such as "The Convent Threshold" emphasize the raw, turbulent and emotional burdens of Medievalist Christianity.

In 1850, John Everett Millais exhibited a painting called "Christ in the House of his Parents," which opened up the Brotherhood to public controversy. Many public figures, including Charles Dickens, attacked Millais for his "ugly" representation of Mary and the depiction of Christ and his family as "alcoholics and slum-dwellers." They criticized the contorted medieval poses as well. Eventually, the Pre-Raphaelite Brotherhood evolved beyond the imitation of medieval art, and all the founders had moved onto a variety of movements and styles by 1860. However, the impact of the Pre-Raphaelite Movement was significant, especially in Great Britain. Many Scottish painters have been influenced by the brotherhood's philosophies. Also, it is widely believed that J.R.R. Tolkien was influenced by the Pre-Raphaelite's mythological images when writing *The Lord of the Rings*. To this day, the Tate Modern in London presents exhibits of Pre-Raphaelite art.

Author of ClassicNote and Sources

Erika Andersen, author of ClassicNote. Completed on August 26, 2013, copyright held by GradeSaver.

Updated and revised A. Boghani November 12, 2013. Copyright held by GradeSaver.

Barringer, Tim. Reading the Pre-Raphaelites. New Haven, CT: Yale University Press, 1998.

Lucinda Hawksley. Essential Pre-Raphaelites. Bath: Dempsey Parr, 1999.

Anthony H. Harrison. "Christina Rossetti in Context." The Victorian Web. 2007-06-24. 2013-08-16. <http://www.victorianweb.org/authors/crossetti/harrison2/5n12.html>.

Anthony H. Harrison. "Pre-Raphaelite Love." The Victorian Web. 2007-06-24. 2013-08-18. <http://www.victorianweb.org/authors/crossetti/harrison2/4.2.html>.

Kate Moller. "Themes of Love in Maude Clare." The Victorian Web. 2003-10-28. 2013-08-19. <http://www.victorianweb.org/authors/crossetti/moller6.html>.

"Maude Clare." 2013-08-24. <http://www.crossref-it.info/textguide/The-poetry-of-Christina-Rossetti/28/1847>.

Hill, Pamela Steed. "Critical Essay on 'Remember'." Poetry for Students. Ed. Anne Marie Hacht. Vol. 14. Detroit: Gale Group, 2002. Literature Resource Center. Web. 24 Aug. 2013.

McSweeney, Kerry. "'What's the Import?': Indefinitiveness of Meaning in Nineteenth-century Parabolic Poems." Style Spring 2002: 36+. Literature Resource Center. Web. 24 August 2013.

Essay: From Objectified to Deified: An Exploration of Self in "Goblin Market"

by Anonymous
December 06, 2005

A torrid lesbian love affair. An acerbic commentary on the commercialization of sex. A dire struggle between physical temptation and spiritual good. A child's nursery rhyme. "Goblin Market" encompasses a wealth of interpretations, some of which smoothly blending together, others remaining diametrically opposed. It symbolizes its creator's complex nature. With each reading, it challenges readers to analyze, debate, and actively engage with it anew. In light of several of her other poems as well as her biography, yet another voice emerges to guide the interpretation of this intricate work. Christina Rossetti's narrative poem "Goblin Market" asserts itself as an early feminist text in its condemnation of the Victorian women's roles and its empowerment of a female heroine. Rossetti denounces her female contemporaries for their characteristic vulnerability and submission to men's wills through her depiction of Laura's temptation and downfall. Rather than merely condemn the status quo, she provides her audience with a credible and inspirational heroine in Lizzie. However, the truly revolutionary and feminist quality of this poem lies in Rossetti's assertion of Lizzie as a female Christ figure. In her contrast between the helpless Laura and the self-reliant Lizzie, Rossetti introduces her Victorian audience to the inevitable shift of women's roles.

The Victim

In the Victorian era, women shouldered the burden of quietly and gratefully attending to their husbands' every need and whim. Rather than retain their own identities, women became men's objects and possessions. In her poem "In an Artist's Studio," Rossetti subtly addresses the injustice of this relationship through her description of a woman objectified in an artist's painting. Instead of portraying her "as she is," the artist merely paints her "as she fills his dreams," without the pains of living that make her human (14). When he represents her simply as a perfect "saint" or "angel," he refuses to acknowledge the "wan with waiting" and dimness of sorrow in a real woman's eyes (7, 12).

Rather than allow Victorian women to add the role of victim to object, Rossetti condemns these women for their inability to assert themselves through her characterization of Laura in "Goblin Market." Despite her initial admonishments to "not look at the goblin men" and "not buy their fruits," Laura finds herself weak-willed and unable to resist their calls (42, 43). "Curious Laura chose to linger" among the goblin men, thereby ignoring her instincts and succumbing to their will (69). Persuasive and assertive in their temptations, they easily crumble her "last restraint" and watch as she "sucked and sucked and sucked the more" (86, 134). Rossetti further chastises women for their weak constitutions in her portrayal of

Laura's helplessness. Upon realizing the futility of her search for the goblin market, Laura "[gnashes] her teeth for baulked desire" and grows as "cold as stone" instead of actively seeking a way to extract herself from these depths of despair (267, 253). Through her tongue-in-cheek portrayal of a woman objectified in a painting coupled with her denunciation of Laura's weakness and helplessness, Rossetti critiques Victorian women's passivity and inferior status in an attempt to propel the recognition of the need for change.

The Heroine

In lieu of demanding instant and revolutionary changes in gender roles, Rossetti offers Victorian women practical and effective means of gaining power. Rather than succumb to the easy solution of a marriage of convenience, the speaker of "'No Thank You, John'" assertively rejects convention in favor of her personal needs. Although many other women "would take pity" on the suitor if he would ask, this woman refuses to "perform that task" because she "never loved" him from the start (9-10, 12, 5). Despite his incessant entreaties, she maintains that she would "rather answer 'No' to fifty Johns" than succumb to weariness and "answer 'Yes' to [him]" (19, 3, 20). Furthermore, the speaker adopts the dominant role when she instructs her immature suitor to "rise above quibbles" and use his "common sense" (29-30, 16).

In addition to her vignette of this speaker creating power for herself, Rossetti further encourages women to challenge the status quo by her portrayal of Lizzie as the heroine in "Goblin Market." Beyond her mere characteristics of purity and kindness, Lizzie's true heroism hails from her active pursuit of danger and her determination to conquer it. As a witness to Laura's anguish, Lizzie fully comprehends the risks of venturing into the world of goblins and forbidden fruit. Despite her desire to "buy fruit to comfort [Laura]," she recalls another girl driven to death by her fall to temptation and fears "to pay too dear" (310, 311). Then Lizzie's wavering ceases when "Laura dwindling seem[s] knocking at Death's door," thereby prompting the heroine to take action (320-321). In order to save Laura, Lizzie begins to actively "listen and look" for danger (328). Though she remains ever mindful of the risk, she firmly demands "much and many" of the fruits and refuses to comply with the goblins' temptation to eat in their presence (365). In both of these poems, Rossetti depicts women who assert their strength and integrity by holding firmly to their principles in the face of temptation.

The Christ-Figure

In her most revolutionary and controversial tactic, Rossetti bolsters the feminist voice of this piece through her portrayal of a female Christ figure. According to her biography, Rossetti embodied many contrasts and polarities as part of her "complex nature" (1611). Deeply devout in her religious beliefs, Rossetti "renounced... any pleasures or relationships that did not conform to her strict Anglo-Catholic principles" (1611). Nevertheless, her life was woven with a thread of defiance of convention in favor of personal integrity: she "regarded her choice of single life as an act of artistic self-preservation" despite the Victorian society's promotion of marriage and procreation as a civic and religious duty (1611). Her ability to reconcile her strict faith with her challenges to convention indicates that she would likewise be capable of toying with controversial aspects of her faith while maintaining the deference for its basic tenets.

In her assertion of Lizzie as a Christ-figure in "Goblin Market," Rossetti simultaneously elevates women's status and empowers them by simply challenging the importance of Christ's gender. Because "tender Lizzie could not bear to watch her sister's cantankerous care" and not "share" in the burden and strife, she parallels Christ's role as the sacrificial lamb (299-300, 301). She willingly offers herself to evil with the intent of rescuing her fallen sister. Just as Christ suffered on the cross to redeem sinners, Lizzie endures the goblins' mauling, mocking and clawing in her attempt to save Laura (429, 401). Despite their taunts and cruelty, "Lizzie [utters] not a word" (430). After the agony and despair, Christ rises from the dead for the salvation of sinners and to inspire his people to spread the word of God's glory. Lizzie likewise transcends the torture of the "evil people" and returns to Laura, for the sake of whom she "braved the glen" (437, 473). By licking the juice residue from Lizzie's face, Laura's anguish lifts and she awakes "as from a dream" and from "life out of death" (537, 524). As Christ's apostles proclaimed his sacrifice, Laura gathers the children to "tell them how her sister stood in deadly peril to do her good" (557-558). In her portrayal of a woman as a Christ-figure, Rossetti further supports a feminist interpretation of this work.

Conclusion

Although she lived in the Victorian era and endured the severe inequality between men and women, Christina Rossetti refused to passively abide by rigid gender roles. The success of her poetic career and her strict professionalism alone attest to her hope for and work towards expanded opportunities for women. In her controversial poem "Goblin Market," Rossetti anticipates a shift in women's roles by contrasting the deeds of Victorian Laura with the early feminist Lizzie. As the embodiment of the Victorian woman, Laura easily succumbs to the goblin men's temptations because of her vulnerability and lack of independence. Lizzie sharply contrasts Laura by resolutely maintaining her moral ground and by coaxing her inner strength to the surface. In an attempt to further challenge these social roles, Rossetti draws distinct connections between the self-sacrifice of the feminist heroine and of Christ. The characterizations of these two women render the "Goblin Market" a feminist work of art. The women of Rossetti's poems span an array of personalities, ranging from a soulless object to a weak-willed sinner to a single woman to a selfless heroine to a Christ-like figure. Through her self-expression in art, Christina Rossetti finally explores the many facets of her "complex nature."

Essay: Freud in the Goblin's Glen

by Anonymous
March 10, 2006

Christina Rossetti's *Goblin Market* beautifully illustrates sin and sacrifice in the lives of twin sisters Lizzie and Laura. These sisters are so alike and separate they can be likened to the ying and yang. It has been argued that they are one person split in two. Because of certain personality traits it can also be argued that these two women represent the subconscious alter egos - the superego and the id. However, while Laura is the id she is also a more fully developed person. Lizzie, being the moral superego, seems little more than Laura's conscience. Lizzie's voice of reason runs through the poem warning the id-like Laura about the goblin men. Laura however must succumb to desire. It is experience of desire and consequence that finally pushes Laura away from the choices of the id, making her a well-rounded person governed not by the pleasure principle, but the reality principle.

Sigmund Freud was the first to identify conscious and unconscious parts of the mind. The mind consists of three parts: the Ego, the Superego, and the Id. The ego is the conscious part of the mind that acts as a balance between the id and the superego.

In Sharon Heller's *Freud A to Z*, she writes the id is "completely submerged in the unconscious ... the id houses the instinctual impulses of sex and aggression and their primal wishes" (90). Furthermore the id is "irrational, timeless, immoral, instinct-driven thought that fails to distinguish fantasy from reality, wish from action" (91). The id personality is hedonistic, and without any regards for others. Guided solely by the pleasure principle, the id seeks instant gratification in all things. The id will do all it can to maximize pleasure and minimize pain.

Laura she is imbued with several of these id-like qualities. She is irrational; without thinking about the consequences "she [clips] a precious golden lock/ [and drops] a tear more rare then a pearl" (127-28), giving a part of herself over to desire. Since the goblins are described as "sly", (96) "leering at each other/.../signaling each other" (93 - 95), the fruits seem like "evil gifts" (66). However, they are described as "luscious" (61) and "fair" (60), "fresh from the vine/...full and fine" (20 -21). They represent sin and desire, making "sweet-[toothed] Laura" (116) immoral when she "[sucks] and [sucks] and [sucks] the more/.../ [Sucks] until her lips [are] sore" (135 - 37). The gluttonous action of eating until it is painful is also sinful, speaking to her desire for gratification and maximum pleasure. She seeks instant gratification; she starts to "[suck] their fruit globes fair or red" (129) as soon as her tear hits the plate. That she is willing to "buy [fruit] from [the goblin men] with a golden curl" (126) shows a lack of acknowledgement of Lizzie's "wise upbraidings" (144). They "must not look at goblin men/.../ [or] their evil gifts [will] harm" (42...67) them.

Like the id, Laura has very little care or concern for those around her. When Laura is looking for the goblin men Lizzie implores, "come Laura, not another maiden lags (224), "let us get home before the night grows dark" (248). She worries "if [they] lost [their] way" (252) they would not know what to do. But without giving care to her sister's fears

Laura [loiters] still among the rushes

And [says] the bank [is] steep.

And ... [that] the hour was early still,

The dew not fall'n, the wind not chill (227-230)

The very act of eating the fruit without caring that "[Lizzie's] light like [Laura's may] be hidden/[Lizzie's] young life like [Laura's may] be wasted" (480-81), is a sign of id-like selfishness. Not that Lizzie would partake, but Laura even forgets to bring back fruit for her, patronizing Lizzy's concerns saying, "have done with sorrow/I'll bring you plumbs tomorrow" (170-71). She does not bring back any fruit for her sister, does not think of her at the time, and is solely interested in her own pleasure and satisfaction.

Yet another way Laura personifies the id is in her dissatisfaction with daily chores. She is always "longing for the night" (215), given the lack of gratification involved. When Laura starts to fade away

She no more [sweeps] the house,

[Tends] the fowls or cows,

[Fetches] honey, [kneads] cakes of wheat,

[Or brings] water from the brook. (293-96)

She leaves everything to Lizzie. Laura only cares that she will "buy no more such dainty fruit/.../ [and find] no more such succous pasture" (257-58).

Lizzie's personality is the polar opposite of Laura's. The superego is our conscience. It "judges, condemns, rewards, and punishes" (92). The superego is also the center of our morality. The ego and the id judge right and wrong based on reward and punishment. The superego internalizes and identifies good and bad, right and wrong, moral and immoral. It maintains social norms, taboos, and cultural values. Where Laura only thinks of herself, Lizzie only thinks of Laura. Laura's goal is instant and self-gratification, Lizzie's is saving her sister. Lizzie is representative of the superego. While the id is instinct, the superego is "a part of the personality that is built up form one's actual experiences" (Heller, 92). Lizzie

...[remembers] Jeanie,

How she met them in the moonlight

...

[and then] pined and pined away;

Sought them by night and day,

Found them no more, but dwindled and grew gray. (148-157)

She learns lessons from what happened to the unfortunate fabled character of Jeanie. As the superego, Lizzie is the embodiment of morality in this poem, "like a lily... [or] a royal virgin" (409-418). She fears and ignores the goblin men, "[thrusting] a dimpled finger/in each ear, [she shuts her] eyes and [runs]" (67-68) from them. She waits until "Laura, dwindling, / [Seems] knocking at Death's door" (320-21). "Lizzie [weighs] no more/better or worse/ [and puts] a penny in her purse" (322-224) and goes to save her sister regardless of her fears.

Like the conscience voice of the superego, Lizzie warns her sister constantly that "[the goblin men's] offers should not charm [them]/ their evil gifts [will] harm [them]" (65-66). She tries to uphold social taboos such as "twilight not [being] good for maidens" (145). Lizzie is the image of the happy homemaker, getting up "when the first cock [crows] his warning" (201), and keeps "like bees ... sweet and busy" (202) holding up that cultural icon as well. In an extreme display of morality "for [Laura's] sake, [Lizzie braves] the glen/and [has] to do with goblin merchant men" (473-74).

However, because she is guided by morality Lizzie seems incapable of becoming an independent well-rounded human being with wants and needs and experience. Desire is seen as negative, thusly Lizzie never acknowledges it. She is the superego, but given her complete lack of experience only seems to be that conscience voice.

In the beginning of the narrative, Laura has a similar apprehension of the fruit merchants that Lizzie does. Laura becomes a more developed person then Lizzie does because she gains experience with it. When the girls are "crouching close together" (36) "among the brook side rushes" (33) Laura, "pricking up her golden head' (41), says:

We must not look at goblin men,

We must not buy their fruits:

Who knows upon what soil they fed

Their hungry thirsty roots. (41-44)

However, Laura does not see the goblin men as "evil people" (437) as Lizzie does. While they are "sly" (96) and seem to seduce Laura with "tones as smooth as honey" (108) she experiences their gifts, for better or worse, not content with the blind innocence, as Lizzie is. Laura does maintain her innocence in a way; she is still likened to Lizzie as they both remain "like two flakes of new-fall'n snow/[or] like two wands of ivory" (189-90). Laura, like Lizzie, is still white and innocent even though she succumbs to desire. It is only when Laura goes "deaf and blind" (259) to desire that she starts to "[dwindle] ... to swift decay" (278-79). The source of desire is taken away from her and she is left with the consequences.

Given that she made the choice to succumb to temptation Laura must live with the consequences. However, this experience and the consequences therein make her a more complete person, pushing her away from the pleasure principle by the end of the narrative. When she has children her "mother-heart [is] beset with fears" (546) showing she cares more for her children than herself. She becomes concerned that Lizzie's life will be "undone in [her] undoing" (482). She accepts blame and seems to accept the consequences. In this, Rossetti might be suggesting that women need to experience desire in some form in order to learn of consequences. Consequences thrust Laura into a more mature place, away from strictly id-based choices, and when she is saved she is able to "[laugh] in the old innocent way" (538). By embracing her sister "twice or thrice" (539) Laura is also embracing her conscience. Women can succumb to desire. They can partly maintain their innocence while gaining valuable experience. So long as their conscience is strong, women can learn from experience, regain their innocence and be better for the experience. Laura chooses to succumb to desire, and through the strength of her conscience sister she stays "like ... flakes of new-fall'n snow" (189) and retains her innocence afterwards.

While Lizzie has internalized the lessons from Jeanie, she cannot hope to be a voice of experience or power when warnings Laura. When she speaks of desire she has no experience with it, only fear of it. Lizzie is "most placid in her look" (217), she is "content ... / [and warbles] for the mere bright day's delight" (212-13) of cooking and cleaning and kneading cakes. She never feels desire throughout the poem because she fears she will "pay too dear" (311). Her constant "wise upbraidings" (142) run through the poem, supporting the idea that she is like the conscience voice that runs through all minds.

After she does save her sister Lizzie seems to fade out of the poem all together. In the last stanza Laura is the only sister named. Lizzie becomes almost obsolete as Laura settles into married life and is no longer driven by the pleasure principle. She has experienced desire and the consequences making her a strong voice of reason. There is a sense that only Laura exists; Laura speaks "about the haunted glen/ [and] the wicked, quaint fruit-merchant men" (552-52) like they are old legends, a fable to scare children away from the choices of the id. Lizzie seems like the brave fabled sister belonging only to the moral of the story:

For there is no friend like a sister

In calm or stormy weather

...

To fetch if one goes astray

...

To strengthen whilst one stands. (561-67)

Laura in effect becomes a real person when previously she was a facet of a personality. Like morality, Lizzie is internalized; the choice between id and superego has been made. Rossetti could be suggesting that women need not fear the choices of the id. Experience is a powerful tool and a way to become well rounded human beings. Laura survives and prospers. Becoming a wife, she has "children of [her] own" (545) and teaches them through story. She has the strength of her conscience, and experience making her a much better voice to "call the little ones/and tell them all of her early prime" (548-49) when she gained her experience. Because of this experience, her "mother-heart beset with fears" (546), and the internalization of Lizzie's morality, Laura lets go of the pleasure principle and becomes a fully developed woman. Lizzie becomes the fabled sister. If Laura remained inexperienced to the consequences of desire she would still be ruled by the pleasure principle as the id.

Laura internalizes Lizzie, the end leaves only one. Laura, the would-be the id eventually turns into the ego, making a complete journey through experience. Lizzie is the superego and the internalized morality. In this poem, as in life, desire has consequences. To fully understand the world, becoming well rounded human beings in it, people must be aloud to understand desire and consequence, either first hand or from a voice of reason.

Works Cited

Heller, Sharon. Freud A to Z. Hoboken, New Jersey. John Wiley & Sons Inc. 2005.

Rossetti, Christina. "Goblin Market". The Longman Anthology of British Literature. 2nd ed. David Damrosch Ed. New York, New York. Pearson Education Inc. 2004. 759 -71.

Quiz 1

1. **Which of these authors was a friend of the Rossetti family?**
   A. Lewis Carroll
   B. Dante Alighieri
   C. Charles Dickens
   D. Emily Dickenson

2. **What was Christina Rossetti's pen name?**
   A. Ellen Alleyne
   B. Silence Dogood
   C. Geoffrey Crayon
   D. Henry Wade

3. **What was the name of the original Pre-Raphaelite journal?**
   A. The Germ
   B. Athenaeum
   C. The Rambler
   D. The Guardian

4. **Which author did Gabriel Rossetti primarily study?**
   A. Vergil
   B. William Shakespeare
   C. Dante Alighieri
   D. Petrarch

5. **What caused Christina Rossetti's death?**
   A. old age
   B. breast cancer
   C. tuberculosis
   D. Graves' disease

6. **What is the relationship between Lizzie and Laura in "Goblin Market"**
   A. mother and daughter
   B. cousins
   C. acquaintances
   D. sisters

7. **Where did Christina Rossetti spend the majority of her life?**
   A. London
   B. Ireland
   C. Italy
   D. France

8. **What was the subject of Christina Rossetti's first poem?**
   A. her father
   B. her older brother
   C. the death of the family pet
   D. a school girl

9. **Why did Christina Rossetti refuse so many offers of marriage?**
   A. She never fell in love
   B. None of the men were rich enough for her
   C. She planned to become a nun
   D. None of them shared her religious views

10. **Which statement about Christina Rossetti is false?**
    A. Christina Rossetti never married
    B. Christina Rossetti grew increasingly famous after her death
    C. Christina Rossetti was not famous in her lifetime
    D. Christina Rossetti suffered from depression

11. **In whose footsteps do scholars believe Rossetti followed?**
    A. Lewis Carroll's
    B. Elizabeth Barrett Browning's
    C. John Keats'
    D. her father's

12. **How many siblings did Rossetti have?**
    A. 2
    B. 3
    C. 4
    D. 5

13. **Fill in the blanks: "We must not ____ ____ goblin men"**
   A. encourage the
   B. speak to
   C. buy from
   D. steal from

14. **What are the goblin men selling?**
   A. golden dishes
   B. exotic spices
   C. beautiful silks
   D. delicious fruit

15. **Who printed Christina Rossetti's first poem?**
   A. James Collinson
   B. her grandfather
   C. her brother Dante
   D. her brother William

16. **Who is the narrator speaking to in "Death's Chill Between"**
   A. God
   B. her father
   C. her mother
   D. her sister

17. **What does sleep often symbolize in Rossetti's poems?**
   A. old age
   B. spiritual inactivity
   C. death
   D. night

18. **Which composer first set "In the Bleak Midwinter" to music?**
   A. R.O. Morris
   B. William Rossetti
   C. Harold Darke
   D. Gustav Holst

19. **What does the inn represent in "Up-Hill"?**
    A. heaven
    B. safety
    C. marriage
    D. financial independence

20. **What is the name of the poetry collection that includes "Baby Lies so Fast Asleep"?**
    A. Goblin Market and Other Poems
    B. The Prince's Progress and Other Poems
    C. Sing-Song
    D. Poems

21. **What is the name of the movement that Christina Rossetti's brothers were involved with?**
    A. Social Gospel movement
    B. Socialism
    C. Pre-Raphaelite movement
    D. Romanticism

22. **Which of the following poems did Christina Rossetti NOT write?**
    A. "Bird Raptures"
    B. "To My Mother"
    C. "De Profundis"
    D. "A Match with the Moon"

23. **In "The Convent Threshold," what does clay symbolize?**
    A. man in relation to God
    B. the mutability of life
    C. life's suffering
    D. sin

24. **Which statement about "Death's Chill Between" is false?**
    A. Rossetti wrote "Death's Chill Between" to soothe her broken heart
    B. "Death's Chill Between" is based on her mother's experiences
    C. The man who Rossetti loved died when she was fifteen
    D. Rossetti did not write "Death's Chill Between" from experience

25. **Why is Maude Clare upset?**

A. she does not love her husband
B. her lover is dead
C. her lover married someone else
D. she does not want to go to church

Quiz 1 Answer Key

1. (**A**) Lewis Carroll
2. (**A**) Ellen Alleyne
3. (**A**) The Germ
4. (**C**) Dante Alighieri
5. (**B**) breast cancer
6. (**D**) sisters
7. (**A**) London
8. (**D**) a school girl
9. (**D**) None of them shared her religious views
10. (**C**) Christina Rossetti was not famous in her lifetime
11. (**B**) Elizabeth Barrett Browning's
12. (**B**) 3
13. (**C**) buy from
14. (**D**) delicious fruit
15. (**B**) her grandfather
16. (**C**) her mother
17. (**C**) death
18. (**D**) Gustav Holst
19. (**A**) heaven
20. (**C**) Sing-Song
21. (**C**) Pre-Raphaelite movement
22. (**D**) "A Match with the Moon"
23. (**A**) man in relation to God
24. (**D**) Rossetti did not write "Death's Chill Between" from experience
25. (**C**) her lover married someone else

Quiz 2

1. **Who is Maude Clare's romantic rival?**
   A. her mother
   B. her sister
   C. Nell
   D. Hetty

2. **What was the original title of "Love Came Down at Christmas"?**
   A. Love All Lovely
   B. Christmastide
   C. A Christmas Sign
   D. Love Divine

3. **What does the title "De Profundis" mean?**
   A. the proficient
   B. deep in thought
   C. from the depths
   D. the profound

4. **When was the Pre-Raphaelite Brotherhood founded?**
   A. 1842
   B. 1845
   C. 1848
   D. 1853

5. **Who is the main character in "De Profundis"?**
   A. God
   B. the angels
   C. Nell
   D. the narrator

6. **Who is the hero in "Goblin Market"?**
   A. Lizzie
   B. Laura
   C. the cat-faced goblin
   D. Jeanie

7. **What are the two types of birds in "Bird Raptures"?**
   A. lark and nightingale
   B. swallow and chickadee
   C. hawk and owl
   D. linnet and sparrow

8. **What was one of Rossetti's inspirations to write "Goblin Market"?**
   A. her sister's life of prostitution
   B. St. Mary Magdalene Home for Fallen Women
   C. Rossetti's personal experience of sexual violence
   D. Rossetti's interest in the fruit trade

9. **What year was Christina Rossetti born?**
   A. 1821
   B. 1830
   C. 1831
   D. 1840

10. **Where did Christina Rossetti's father teach?**
   A. King's College
   B. Oxford
   C. in his home
   D. Italy

11. **What caused Christina Rossetti's depression as a teenager?**
   A. her isolation
   B. her lack of good looks
   C. verbal abuse from her mother
   D. she could not read

12. **When was "Goblin Market" published?**
   A. 1847
   B. 1862
   C. 1863
   D. 1876

13. **What wedding gift does Maude Clare give to Sir Thomas and Nell?**
   A. her half of a golden chain
   B. a beautiful pocket watch
   C. a bouquet of lilies
   D. her blessing

14. **What advice does Thomas' mother give him in "Maude Clare"?**
   A. that his marriage will endure Maude Clare's sneers
   B. that he should not marry Nell or Maude
   C. that he should accept the golden chain
   D. that he should marry Maude Clare instead

15. **What is the silent land in "Remember"?**
   A. home
   B. Italy
   C. death
   D. sleep

16. **Who undertook the task of educating Christina Rossetti?**
   A. her father
   B. her mother
   C. her sister
   D. a governess

17. **What are Christina Rossetti's two most famous narrative poems?**
   A. "Maude Clare" and "In the Bleak Midwinter"
   B. "De Profundis" and "Bird Raptures"
   C. "Goblin Market" and "The Prince's Progress"
   D. "Remember" and "Up-Hill"

18. **Who was Christina Rossetti's maternal grandfather?**
   A. a friend and physician of Lord Byron
   B. a relative of Charles Dickens
   C. a carpenter from Italy
   D. a famous political exile

19. **What does Laura give the goblin men as payment for the fruit?**
   A. her first child
   B. her finest clothes
   C. a lock of hair
   D. golden coins

20. **Who is the Christ figure in "Goblin Market"?**
   A. Lizzie
   B. Nell
   C. Laura
   D. Jeanie

21. **What happens to those who eat the goblin men's fruit?**
   A. they die immediately
   B. they become immortal
   C. they cannot hear the call of goblin men and die from pining
   D. they are not harmed

22. **Why did Gabriele Rossetti stop his teaching job?**
   A. the Rossetti family become very wealthy
   B. deteriorating health
   C. he was lazy
   D. he was fired

23. **Who often painted imges of Christina Rossetti?**
   A. Dante Rossetti
   B. James Collinson
   C. William Rossetti
   D. Gabriele Rossetti

24. **Where do Lizzie and Laura live in "Goblin Market"?**
   A. in a castle
   B. in a small cottage
   C. in the woods
   D. with the goblin men

25. **What was the original title of "Goblin Market"?**

A. "Laura's Blunder"
B. "A Look at Goblin Men"
C. "A Peep at the Goblins"
D. "Goblin Wares"

Quiz 2 Answer Key

1. **(C)** Nell
2. **(B)** Christmastide
3. **(C)** from the depths
4. **(C)** 1848
5. **(D)** the narrator
6. **(A)** Lizzie
7. **(A)** lark and nightingale
8. **(B)** St. Mary Magdalene Home for Fallen Women
9. **(B)** 1830
10. **(A)** King's College
11. **(A)** her isolation
12. **(B)** 1862
13. **(A)** her half of a golden chain
14. **(A)** that his marriage will endure Maude Clare's sneers
15. **(C)** death
16. **(B)** her mother
17. **(C)** "Goblin Market" and "The Prince's Progress"
18. **(A)** a friend and physician of Lord Byron
19. **(C)** a lock of hair
20. **(A)** Lizzie
21. **(C)** they cannot hear the call of goblin men and die from pining
22. **(B)** deteriorating health
23. **(A)** Dante Rossetti
24. **(B)** in a small cottage
25. **(C)** "A Peep at the Goblins"

Quiz 3

1. **Which of the following is NOT a possible interpretation of the journey in "Up-hill"?**
   A. life after death
   B. life
   C. death
   D. adolescence

2. **Why can't Sir Thomas speak to Maude Clare?**
   A. He's awed by her beauty
   B. He's too busy with his mother
   C. Nell doesn't want him to
   D. He's embarrassed

3. **How many characters speak in "Up-Hill"?**
   A. 1
   B. 2
   C. 3
   D. 4

4. **Pre-Raphaelite writing is often described as...?**
   A. word-painting
   B. based in reality
   C. unfeeling
   D. dancing with words

5. **Why did William Rossetti dismiss his sister's adolescent autobiography?**
   A. He was jealous
   B. He called it immature
   C. His sister falsified most of the information
   D. It went against the Pre-Raphaelite Brotherhood

6. **Where is Christina Rossetti buried?**
   A. Abney Park
   B. in a pauper's grave
   C. Highgate Cemetary
   D. Westminster Abbey

7. **In the 1840s, what caused financial troubles for the Rossetti family?**
   A. Christina Rossetti's father's ill health
   B. unsuccessful speculation
   C. Christina Rossetti's mother's death
   D. lavish lifestyle

8. **Out of the following, the most common theme in Christina Rossetti's poetry is...**
   A. mythology
   B. child birth
   C. birds
   D. religious contemplation

9. **Which of Christina Rossetti's poems is most commonly read in schools?**
   A. "Goblin Market"
   B. "Bird Raptures"
   C. "To My Mother"
   D. "De Profundis"

10. **What are Lizzie and Laura's main activities in "Goblin Market"?**
   A. selling fruit
   B. they do no work
   C. visiting friends
   D. housework and farm chores

11. **To whom are Lizzie and Laura telling their story in "Goblin Market"?**
   A. their friends
   B. their children
   C. their husbands
   D. Jeanie

12. **What is the moral lesson at the end of "Goblin Market"?**
   A. "Money is the root of all evil"
   B. "Never talk to strangers"
   C. "There is no friend like a sister"
   D. "Do not be a glutton"

13. **In "Goblin Market," where do the goblin men sell their wares?**
    A. in town
    B. in caves
    C. from door to door
    D. by the river

14. **In "Goblin Market," what do the goblins try to force Lizzie to do?**
    A. drink the juice of the fruit
    B. kill Laura
    C. give them her hair
    D. give them her money

15. **What famous Biblical scene does "In the Bleak Midwinter" portray?**
    A. the nativity of Christ
    B. Adam and Eve
    C. Moses' birth
    D. the death of Christ

16. **In "In the Bleak Midwinter," what are Cherubim and seraphim?**
    A. angels
    B. demons
    C. sisters
    D. the names of the cows in the stable

17. **How many lines does a sonnet typically contain?**
    A. 6
    B. 12
    C. 14
    D. 16

18. **Complete this sentence: Christina Rossetti's poems _____ have a rhyme a scheme.**
    A. always
    B. occasionally
    C. almost always
    D. never

19. **When did "Goblin Market" come to the forefront of scholarly study?**
    A. immediately after its publication
    B. in the late 20th century
    C. in the early 21st century
    D. right after Christina Rossetti's death

20. **In "Love Came Down at Christmas", what does Godhead mean?**
    A. God the father
    B. the Holy Spirit
    C. the Trinity
    D. Jesus

21. **What does "repentance" mean?**
    A. return to sin
    B. asking forgiveness
    C. showing mercy
    D. paying one's debt

22. **Complete this sentence: Christina Rossetti wrote fairy tales____**
    A. with children
    B. inspired by children's dreams
    C. at children
    D. for children

23. **What was the Pre-Raphaelite movement?**
    A. The movement in art influenced by Raphael's work
    B. a mid 19th century reform movement in art in England
    C. an 18th century political movement in England
    D. a philanthropic drive to rehabilitate prostitutes

24. **Who lived in the St. Mary Magdalene Home?**
    A. Anglican nuns
    B. Christina Rossetti's sister
    C. fallen women
    D. Christina Rossetti

25. **Why did Rossetti choose to write about infant death?**

A. she wished for the death of her own infant

B. infant death was common in the Victorian era

C. it made an interesting subject

D. she did not love children

Quiz 3 Answer Key

1. **(D)** adolescence
2. **(D)** He's embarrassed
3. **(B)** 2
4. **(A)** word-painting
5. **(B)** He called it immature
6. **(C)** Highgate Cemetary
7. **(A)** Christina Rossetti's father's ill health
8. **(D)** religious contemplation
9. **(A)** "Goblin Market"
10. **(D)** housework and farm chores
11. **(B)** their children
12. **(C)** "There is no friend like a sister"
13. **(D)** by the river
14. **(A)** drink the juice of the fruit
15. **(A)** the nativity of Christ
16. **(A)** angels
17. **(C)** 14
18. **(A)** always
19. **(B)** in the late 20th century
20. **(A)** God the father
21. **(B)** asking forgiveness
22. **(C)** at children
23. **(B)** a mid 19th century reform movement in art in England
24. **(C)** fallen women
25. **(B)** infant death was common in the Victorian era

Quiz 4

1. **Which of the following poems is a sonnet?**
    A. Goblin Market
    B. In the Bleak Midwinter
    C. Remember
    D. Baby lies so fast asleep

2. **Which famous novel was inspired by "Goblin Market"?**
    A. Charles Dickens' Bleak House
    B. Lewis Carroll's Alice's Adventures in Wonderland
    C. Elizabeth Barrett Browning's The Battle of Marathon
    D. Christina Rossetti's childhood memoir

3. **What does "incarnate" mean?**
    A. carnal
    B. fiercely
    C. insatiable
    D. in the flesh

4. **What does "purloin" mean?**
    A. to delay
    B. to cook something well
    C. to wonder
    D. to steal something

5. **How many of Christina Rossetti's poems were printed in The Germ?**
    A. 2
    B. 7
    C. 9
    D. 16

6. **Which publication first printed Christina Rossetti's work?**
    A. The Athenaeum
    B. The Germ
    C. The Times
    D. The Weekly Journal

7. **Which branch of Christianity did Christina Rossetti practice?**
   A. Tractarianism
   B. Anabaptism
   C. Roman Catholicism
   D. Puritanism

8. **Which statement about Christina Rossetti's religion is false?**
   A. She practiced her mother's religion
   B. Christina practiced her father's religion
   C. Christina was a devout Christian
   D. She refused offers of marriage for religious reasons

9. **Who is the narrator in "Remember"?**
   A. just a narrator
   B. a young man
   C. a young wife
   D. probably Rossetti

10. **Which statement about Christina Rossetti's romantic life is false?**
   A. Rossetti was never engaged
   B. She was prone to melancholy
   C. She was extremely shy
   D. She was proposed to by three men

11. **What was Christina Rossetti's cultural heritage?**
   A. German
   B. French Italian
   C. English French
   D. English Italian

12. **What does 'Rossetti' mean?**
   A. the rose
   B. hot-headed
   C. of the land
   D. little red

13. **What is the month in which Christina Rossetti was born and died?**
    A. January
    B. December
    C. February
    D. September

14. **Why was Gabriele Rossetti exiled from Italy?**
    A. he wrote against the papacy
    B. he killed a prominent leader
    C. he was not exiled, he left voluntarily
    D. he supported the revolutionary party

15. **What device does the narrator of "Death's Chill Between" use to speak to her dead lover?**
    A. trochee
    B. embellishment
    C. epiphany
    D. apostrophe

16. **What is the common rhyme scheme for ballads?**
    A. ABAB
    B. ABCB
    C. AABB
    D. ABBA

17. **What genre of literature is "Up-Hill"?**
    A. romance
    B. epic narrative
    C. devotional
    D. epistolary

18. **How many issues of The Germ were published?**
    A. 3
    B. 4
    C. 60
    D. it continues today

19. **Which of these answers is TRUE?**
    A. Christina Rossetti was not an important part of the Pre-Raphaelite Movement
    B. Christina Rossetti remains a popular poet today
    C. Christina Rossetti believed that fame would bring her happiness
    D. Christina Rossetti was not published until after her death

20. **When was "A Birthday" published?**
    A. 1848
    B. 1859
    C. 1861
    D. 1865

21. **What day does "A Birthday" represent?**
    A. Christina Rossetti's death
    B. Christina Rossetti's own birthday
    C. Christina Rossetti's father's birthday
    D. The second coming of Christ

22. **What is the name of the device that Rossetti uses when repeating "My heart" in "A Birthday"?**
    A. anaphora
    B. enjambment
    C. apostrophe
    D. zugma

23. **Who is the narrator in "A Birthday"?**
    A. God
    B. her father
    C. a young girl
    D. Christina Rossetti

24. **Which statement is false?**
    A. Christina Rossetti is read widely
    B. Christina Rossetti is known for her poetry
    C. Christina Rossetti excelled at composing sonnets
    D. Christina Rossetti's fairy tales are her best-selling work

25. **Which of the following is NOT true about the Pre-Raphaelite Movement?**

A. It often portrayed historical subjects

B. It was abstract

C. It favored clarity and detail

D. It was influenced by Quatrrocento Italian Art

Quiz 4 Answer Key

1. **(C)** Remember
2. **(B)** Lewis Carroll's Alice's Adventures in Wonderland
3. **(D)** in the flesh
4. **(D)** to steal something
5. **(B)** 7
6. **(A)** The Athenaeum
7. **(A)** Tractarianism
8. **(B)** Christina practiced her father's religion
9. **(D)** probably Rossetti
10. **(A)** Rossetti was never engaged
11. **(D)** English Italian
12. **(D)** little red
13. **(B)** December
14. **(D)** he supported the revolutionary party
15. **(D)** apostrophe
16. **(A)** ABAB
17. **(C)** devotional
18. **(B)** 4
19. **(B)** Christina Rossetti remains a popular poet today
20. **(C)** 1861
21. **(D)** The second coming of Christ
22. **(A)** anaphora
23. **(D)** Christina Rossetti
24. **(D)** Christina Rossetti's fairy tales are her best-selling work
25. **(B)** It was abstract

ClassicNotes

GradeSaver™

Getting you the grade since 1999™

Other ClassicNotes from GradeSaver™

Fight Club
Fight Club (Film)
Flags of Our Fathers
Flannery O'Connor's Stories
Flight
For Whom the Bell Tolls
Founding Brothers
The Fountainhead
Frankenstein
Franny and Zooey
The Giver
The Glass Castle
The Glass Menagerie
The God of Small Things
The Godfather
Goethe's Faust
The Good Earth
The Good Woman of Setzuan
Gorilla, My Love
The Grapes of Wrath
Great Expectations
The Great Gatsby
Grendel
The Guest
Gulliver's Travels
Hamlet
The Handmaid's Tale
Hard Times
Haroun and the Sea of Stories
Harry Potter and the Philosopher's Stone
Heart of Darkness
Hedda Gabler
Henry IV (Pirandello)
Henry IV Part 1
Henry IV Part 2
Henry V
Herzog
Hippolytus
The History of Tom Jones, a Foundling
The Hobbit
Homo Faber
The Hound of the Baskervilles
The House of Bernarda Alba
House of Mirth
The House of the Seven Gables
The House of the Spirits
House on Mango Street
How the Garcia Girls Lost Their Accents
Howards End
A Hunger Artist
The Hunger Games
I Know Why the Caged Bird Sings
I, Claudius
An Ideal Husband
Iliad
The Importance of Being Earnest
In Cold Blood
In Our Time
In the Skin of a Lion
In the Time of the Butterflies
Incidents in the Life of a Slave Girl
Inherit the Wind
An Inspector Calls
Interpreter of Maladies
Into the Wild
Invisible Man
Ishmael
The Island of Dr. Moreau
Jane Eyre
Jazz
The Jew of Malta
Johnny Tremain
Joseph Andrews
A Journal of the Plague Year
The Joy Luck Club
Jude the Obscure
Julius Caesar
The Jungle
Jungle of Cities
Kama Sutra
Kate Chopin's Short Stories
Kidnapped
King Lear
King Solomon's Mines
The Kite Runner
The Lais of Marie de France
Lancelot: Or, the Knight of the Cart
Last of the Mohicans
Le Morte d'Arthur
Leaves of Grass
Legend

For our full list of over 250 Study Guides, Quizzes,
Sample College Application Essays, Literature Essays and E-texts, visit:

www.gradesaver.com

25180603R00066

Printed in Great Britain
by Amazon